Awakening
——TO——
ANGELIC WISDOM

A GUIDE TO SPIRITUAL
CHANNELED COMMUNICATION

LINDSAY S GODFREE

Awakening to Angelic Wisdom
A Guide to Spiritual Channeled Communication

ISBN: 979-8-9903528-1-0

Book Design: Transcendent Publishing
Editor: Susan Free
Photography: Lindsay Godfree
Biblical references: King James Version

The author of this publication does not provide medical, psychological, or other professional advice. The information presented is for educational and informational purposes only and should not be used as a substitute for professional diagnosis, treatment, or guidance. Readers are encouraged to consult qualified professionals for any health, mental, or other concerns. Because of the dynamic nature of the internet, any websites or links referenced in this book or its bibliography may have changed or may no longer be available.

Printed in the United States of America.

Allow yourself to be lifted up,
to fly above the radar of what the mind knows
into the great beyond of PEACE, LOVE, JOY,
and follow THAT rainbow HOME.

The Angels

CONTENTS

INTRODUCTION

*W*hen I felt I could no longer go on in life, I surrendered to asking for divine direction. I followed answers that felt like intuitive nudging, carefully taking small and inspired actions, eventually leading to receiving messages from the realms of the angels. I was intrigued, curious, and scared; I was resistant to what would change if I listened to and acted on the divine direction I received. What would it mean in my life? What would change, and who would I be?

I have been communicating with angels for years now, and it still surprises and delights me. This is my story of how it all began:

In a Unity Church, I met a man named Michael who was leading meditations there. He was a healer and someone I trusted. In a class we were taking together, he asked me if I knew how blessed I was. I said no, I did not, a little taken aback. At that time, I felt lost, continually seeking ways to soothe my soul. He told me that Archangel Michael was standing there with me, and I would be well-known one day. The idea of being in the spotlight freaked me out. I didn't want to be well-known or have notoriety since I am an introvert; I just wanted to help quietly with the conscious awakening happening on Earth.

In 2014, I experienced a spiritual "awakening" to the divinity within each of us. It was a dimensional shift to experiencing the Oneness of everything without fear and a deep knowing of everything as perfect. I asked Spirit how I could integrate it into daily life. I followed my intuition step by step and was curious about channeling; I was "activated as a channel" for angels, writing what I could feel and know from a higher source.

I feared what others might think and say about me as someone who "talks to angels." But then I worried that they might stop. Angels have continued to speak to me, and I love receiving and writing their messages regularly. Their messages are expansive, healing, and even prophetic. You may be surprised by what the angels want to say to us—I know I am. I believe angels are here to help us make a difference and bring a loving presence to our world that sometimes seems so unforgiving.

I am motivated to be of service to help bring a new age of love and peace to our world. My spiritual awakening happened as I developed practices that helped me to recover from being too depressed to move forward in life. I felt I had messed up my life so much that it could never be fixed, felt broken inside, and had no clue as to how to self-correct. I threw myself at the mercy of God/Source/the Universe and vowed to follow whatever guidance I received from a Higher Source.

Life certainly has taken on entirely expanded new dimensions since that time. To come out of my extreme depression, I went through a process of forgiving myself at deep levels for my mistakes, including forgiving feelings of abandonment by God and

Spirit. I now believe that we are all part of an infinite creator, a field of consciousness that holds an eternal and expanding oneness, which I often call ALL THAT IS. I practiced gratitude for the little things. I prayed for hours daily for grace and healing for the sick and dying at the hospital where I worked. The culmination came with feelings of being overwhelmed by an experience of blissful happiness and a sublime connection to ALL THAT IS. I could only laugh and cry in spasms.

I documented this story in my first book, *Awakening Consciousness: Discovering a Larger Version of Self*. I felt one with God/Source/the Universe, knowing that nothing was wrong or broken—a Higher Self orchestrated everything that led to this reunion. I was left with a greater understanding of my life's journey. I realized that everything that had happened in my life had been "perfect" because it brought me to this knowing. That realization turned my world inside out and upside down.

Since then, I have tried to listen and follow step-by-step the intuitive guidance given to me daily. Some days, I can only take small steps toward my goal of sharing the bliss of full connection with the Universe again. I want to share with everyone the oneness of unity consciousness. I still practice my intuition and connection to guidance as much as possible each day. One of those intuitive prompts led me to take an in-person course on channeling—a subject I had never been interested in pursuing. But I had a persistent, intuitive feeling that I was meant to go. The channeled messages for this book started on that first day of class when the participants in the room were "activated as channels." Somehow, all I needed was this permission to connect, and I am giving you that "permission" to talk with the angelic realms yourself.

This journey with the angels is a valuable tool you can also use in your awakening process.

The class challenge was to continue automatic writing every day for a month. It was so enjoyable that I continued automatic handwritten downloads for over a year, collecting them in notebooks, thinking they wouldn't interest anyone. Truthfully, I hardly read them before putting them in my "to-do's" pile for later and filing them away. Eventually, the messages became so profound and timely that I couldn't help but share them. After several years, I began including more and more of them in my blog, the *Consciousness Guide*, which I used to document my spiritual journey for years.

I start this book with the first powerful message so that you, dear reader, can see why I continue to reach out to receive and write the messages. I also included some of the first personal channels encouraging me to continue. I must occasionally remind myself why I am doing this, and I want to give you an honest feeling of what my journey with the angel guides has been, so you might feel inspired and apply their messages to your journey to happiness as well. Being in their frequencies of love, support, admiration, and all aspects of the divine is life-changing.

Archangel Gabriel and other angels and archangels are relentless in their efforts to awaken us to our higher selves. They kept encouraging me, and I believe their messages also apply to you since we are all one as "children of God." Now, I don't write my blog posts anymore. Angels are much more interesting to me.

The angels offer boundless love, encouragement, and empathetic prodding to all who will listen. Over the years, I have collected many readers and am releasing the first previously unpublished messages in this book to encourage you to be all you can be.

I offer the profound messages that I call *Angel-Oracle Messages* to you as support in your life, as guidance infused with light and love. I believe that energy transmissions of love and light are included within the messages that uplift us to a higher consciousness. They uplift and inspire us with healing and often prophetic messages.

I pray that you will find communication with angelic energies as comforting, inspirational, enlightening, and full of love as I do. I pass the love on to you that came in loud and clear in the first angel message:

I love you, and Heaven loves you mightily!

WHY YOU BENEFIT FROM WORKING WITH ANGELS

*W*orking with the angels offers many incredible benefits. Do you have a working relationship with angels and other spirit guides? You could, and I do believe that we should.

You may wonder who they are anyway. Maybe you have never been properly introduced to angels. For some, they are merely fairy tales.

They are so much more than "fairies who locate parking places," just hanging around waiting to find our car keys or stepping in when we need protection from "dark forces."

Angels have profound, energetic blessings to bestow upon us.

There are reasons why angels and archangels have appeared to mankind since the beginning of time. Called the messengers of God, archangels are energetic light beings who vibrate at the frequencies of the attributes of God/Source.

These frequencies correspond energetically to the twelve light rays of color and are historically portrayed as twelve major archangels. These twelve attributes of God are vortexes of light that resonate at light frequencies and correspond to sounds and mathematical codes. The Bible speaks of many kinds and choirs of angels; different cultures have other angelic interventions, and more angels are being created to meet the infinite imagination of the spirit.

How to Use This Book

To get the most benefit from this book, realize that the words in these writings are secondary to the powerful and direct transmissions of the frequency of love within them. These transmissions consist primarily of seventh-dimensional angelic frequencies laced with Christ-Light and the I AM presence of your own being. These are not alien to us but, from an eternal energy perspective, are multidimensional layers of our higher self.

Each Angel-Oracle Message contains powerful energy transmissions directly from angels and archangels. These beings of light are always ready and eager to assist with a boost to your light and help smooth the rough roads of life. Each message contains a powerful download to your light body. (Please note that the angel messages are set in an italic font throughout the book. Thoughts from me within the body of the messages are set off in parentheses.)

Together, these transmissions act as an open gateway of transformation; you only need to step through it. Consciously walking through this gateway with the angels in this way is embarking on a journey into heavenly realms where you will receive what you need to hear most: love, comfort, peace, clarity, and guidance.

Connecting to the messengers that embody divine light is an initiation on the path that leads to embodying the highest divine truth of being. There is no better time to step into this journey than now. Because your attention is here, know that this book has appeared as the next step in your awakening.

Allow yourself time and space to reflect upon and integrate the light frequency of each chapter. Listen to your inner guidance and discernment to determine how much time and space you need to process between transmissions. Honor your intuition to feel what parts of the messages are relevant to you at this time and move on from those that are not.

This might mean you read one message each day or one chapter per week. The important thing is to allow yourself the gift of being fully present with each energetic message rather than trying to rush through reading the entire collection in one sitting. It takes time to assimilate this much light/love, and too much can precipitate uncomfortable reactions.

I have included eight tools at the end of the chapters to help you connect and communicate with the angels awaiting your turning toward them for assistance. It is their joy to help you however they can, without taking away your sovereignty and choices.

As you read these Angel-Oracle Messages, imagine that you are in the direct presence of angels. Imagine that they are speaking to you through the words and also directly through a stream of higher consciousness, higher light, and elevated frequency. Feel your oneness with this consciousness.

Pay attention to your subtle senses and feelings as you feel, sense, know, listen to, and read the guidance to help you develop your personal relationship with the energies of heaven, known as angels. Much of what is being conveyed in these transmissions is on a level beyond words that transforms your cellular structures and activates your crystal-light body. It is important to drink plenty of water to enable you to hold this light/love and get more rest.

Know that angelic presence will connect with you directly on many levels, both during and beyond time, because you are actively reading the transmissions. Pay attention to your dreams, meditations, and the synchronicities that unfold in your life, as these are areas where these teachings can be unpacked and used practically. Mindfulness and attention to all the subtle realms of being that are part of us and our experience as humans expand life to more joy.

As you read, allow your awareness to relax, enter within, and be open to the love that is available here to lift you above the state of your ordinary mental consciousness. Let yourself lift into an awareness and perception of higher divine intelligence as you allow the divine light to support you in unlocking your perception at the level of the divine mind.

Ask Archangel Michael specifically to protect you from any "negative" energies and the vibration of fear. He is the archangel who watches over and supports our divine plans on Earth. He is a powerful vortex and higher-dimensional being who can simultaneously be with all who call upon him. He is the armor of God, often pictured surrounded by blue light, with a shield and sword of flame.

You are encouraged to engage directly on a multidimensional level with Archangel Michael, who transcends space and time.

With awareness of his energy, you may notice greater love and angelic energy overflowing into all areas of your life.

After reading this book, you can also use it as an oracle. Open it with the intention of finding the perfect transmission and message that will most serve you at the time. Open your heart to fully receive the gifts within the messages.

Now is the time to unlock the divine intelligence, wisdom, love, and frequency available to you. Angels have always been present, ready, willing, and able to assist you in embodying all that you are. How much you get out of this book will directly relate to how much you are willing to allow. It is correlated to the awareness and presence you bring to it.

There is an immense opportunity now to let go of your burdens, to surrender any doubt and fears that come up in your mind, and to boldly step into the stream of love available to support you on your journey to live your most uplifted and glorious life.

With love and light,

Lindsay

1
BEGINNINGS

The Gift of Clairaudient Channeling
Awakens in Me

*A*fter I vowed to make my decisions in life only after following intuitive promptings from Spirit, I began living a much happier life. As stated earlier, I followed one such prompt when I attended Marilyn's channeling course, even though I had no particular interest in being a channeler. During class, Marilyn performed an activation to awaken our abilities and instructed us to begin to write. The idea was to quiet the mind, just to put pen to paper and let the information flow through without editing. This technique is called *automatic writing*.

The mind wants to stay in control and interpret everything to align with its comfort zone of previous understanding, so the key to learning to get messages is to listen to the Soulful Self and messages from higher states of consciousness. Since receiving that first message, my journey with the Angel-Oracle messages has worked in amazing and powerful ways.

My guidance has been primarily from the angelic realm. Sometimes, they identify themselves as specific angels and archangels, but often speak as a collective. They continue to surprise and delight me, and inspire and encourage me.

I am honored to share these beautiful messages with you. They include transmissions, activations, and blessings to upgrade our vibration and consciousness. My website features additional weekly messages, in addition to my YouTube channel. The messages included in this book are not published anywhere else. Refer to the last section at the end of the book for more information.

Since I began writing, I have learned that we are all channels of divine energy, and the interpretation of that energy is revealed daily in our life experiences. Anyone can learn to channel; it only takes attunement to the vibrational frequency. I hope my interpretation of divine energy is as uplifting and transformative for you as it has been for me.

Note: The channeled messages appear in italics so you know when they are channeled as angel messages and when the writing is mine alone.

First Channeled Message

As I received my first channeled message, I noticed that a rush of energy rose through me. I felt it in the energetic roots that I anchored to the core center of the earth during the prayer and guided meditation of the group attending the class. The energy rose through my core, and I felt it move out of my hands.

My unspoken question was, "What do my guides want me to know?" I emptied my mind and listened. Poised with a pen to a blank sheet of paper, the following words began to flow quickly and deliberately onto the page with immense energy. The words came pouring out without my knowing what I was writing.

I AM Mighty! I AM in tune with the Holy Spirit. I AM one with ALL THAT IS.

(I heard this in a booming voice and I asked it within my mind, "What is the most important thing that I need to know?" And the answer came.)

The activation is taking place. The cells are changing into the new human. The light zips around the body, and the body loves this new happiness.

As you surrender to the process and allow, the information will unfold. The voice of the "Mighty I AM" will be heard and felt, received, and anchored in the physical.

There is nothing that can withstand the light that is pouring in.

Allow—allow—AWAKEN!

I was stunned. This first message was short, but I was blown away by the power of what was written on the paper. As I read the message, I thought, "Wow, this definitely was NOT written by me!" I didn't experience myself as mighty in any way, shape, or form. I had not expected that kind of instant connection at all. Marilyn, personified as her guide Adaronda, walked through the crowd; taking my hands, she said, "Do not do this channeling while you are driving." I was again shocked, "How did she know I was a longhaul truck driver?" I thought.

On the day I took the Channeling Course and realized I could get messages, I failed miserably at the other psychic exercises but took to heart the challenge to do automatic writing every day for a month.

The next day, I received the following message from my angelic voice.

Ask and Ye Shall Receive

Ask and ye shall receive is the theme of the day—and of the year, and perhaps your lifetime.

Fear of asking and receiving "no" as an answer has been just as potent as the fear of your wildest dreams coming to pass. As you know, fear does not serve you.

It is not about whether or not you get a yes or no—it's about getting clarity of your intention and connecting to happiness.

It is good to feel excited. Like being in love, there is a thrill that makes one giggle with anticipation. Anticipate the best for yourself and, for that matter, everyone else, too. Get excited—run, dance, and shout if you need to. It's fun. Have fun!

The habit of holding it all in does not serve. Let all energy flow. Breathe in, and out, and through.

The trajectory of the future has shifted, though obscure, and is the point of beginning. Each choice is pivotal. One knows not whether that choice is the one, that made all the difference. Not to worry, little ones—each step is an adventure, and all leads to home in oneness as Source.

Be rocked in the arms of the Divine Mother. You are safe in the world of form.

The Angels

The preceding message struck me as relevant to many of us who identify as light bearers and light bringers, love workers and healers, on the path of doing good and awakening consciousness. We all yearn to be held in the arms of the mother energies to feel safe, seen, and loved, whether we admit it or not. Cool! I get to have messages that are relevant to humanity. "This will be fun!" I thought. The angels even told me to have fun.

Later, I received the following personal message from Archangel Gabriel regarding my writing. I share it with you here so you can relate to what I was going through as I received direction. We are all called to receive our direction and power directly from God/ Source/ Universal Consciousness. I couldn't quite process what was happening, nor could I deny it.

The Heavens Open: Archangel Gabriel

The heavens open. You cannot put it off any longer. The pressure of Source energy will not be denied expression on Earth, as it is in Heaven.

Do not try to stop or edit the flow. Only write. Your time has come. Write!

The heavens open, and all is known—the veil becomes transparent.

You were born for this eventuality. Your life experience has set up the scenario for the victory. It WILL NOT be denied! You will not be denied the fullness of your true Self, which stands over you. Integrate this!

Time is not. The Now is here. Be present in it. There is power behind the birth. The birth canal is full, and the pressure of that birth is imminent. Make room at the inn. The manger will receive the Christ child. Make way!

You cannot resist. It only creates pain. Celebrate. Sing hosanna in the highest. It is a miracle taking form, with a life of its own. You are separate from that life, but not. Yes, you feel the oneness—you feel the energy in the womb of being. Accept that it is come.

Do not fear. There is only joy in the becoming and the suckling of that new life—ready to grow up. (This is highly embarrassing, but I felt the energy spin the chakras in my breasts—a little weird—okay, a lot weird!)

You can do naught else at this time. Your entire energy system is poised to give birth to your creative gifts. Just do not resist the contractions of spirit. Your body knows how to birth even the crystal-light body that comes through into being.

Relax into it. Breathe.

(My body goes into a breathing meditation of its own accord. More weirdness.)

Gabriel announces this birth!

It is done!

(Thank you! I think, "I AM GRATEFUL," as the angel, through my hand, draws a heart on the page. I believe the message is over, but then it continues. I think, "Oh my gosh, now they even drew pictures with my hand? What's next?")

Your body burns with the fire of the Holy Spirit—that part of the trinity that represents knowingness. It flows through and bounces back from Mother Earth for the edification of all.

Keep anchoring it in all of you. The result will be more than you can imagine. The New Earth supports the "new human" spoken of by many spiritual leaders at this time.

You wonder how the Earth and humanity will change and how fast this can happen. It is one by one, each individual and each choice, that upgrades the collective.

And yes, from the divine perspective, there is no linear time, so your perception of the time it will take is not a question that can be answered. It takes as long as it takes for each individual to awaken.

And yes, you could relax and have fun with it. (I must be asking questions in my head that are being answered.) *We know it is exciting and you are afraid to celebrate prematurely. And yet the celebration is the priming of the pump of creating the flow of events—it is a conundrum.*

The questions in your mind have been answered. You know the answers, and like many, you still ask again. All is well, little one—you are heard, seen, and not forgotten. Your own Self is a fragment of the answer you seek.

I will be more specific about what YOU can do. **Write for those who are, and who will be, confused.** *You can bring clarity to the ideas that seem complex to many. You know this. Do not delay in writing your messages to the world. It is good that you at least start in this way to daily let Source energy flow through you and find words to put on the paper that can be shared.*

Words are a matrix that frames the concepts into manifestation—as you are already aware. Use them, and love them into being real as they align with the expansion of consciousness. Many will find comfort in them.

What will bring them comfort? Always they need to hear how dearly they are loved and that you/they all can receive that love at will, if only you will allow it. Free will and God's will—no resistance. How great is that? Imagine it now.

What will your writing do? It will provide cups for energy transmission, and you need not worry so much about the content because the content is not yours— it is light energy, and as you know, the important message is within the spaces. That is rather hilarious (the words don't even matter), *don't you think?*

Stay the course—all will be revealed in the fullness of time in the pregnant pauses.

You do not have the full picture yet; it will unfold daily. Continue to write, and the answers will become more detailed and more succinct. You, too, can be the vessel, for oneness is full to overflowing with the wine of goodness and mercy.

It is giving unto all like rainwater for the blooming of the prophecies and the hopes of the messengers in all ages and dimensions. Is it not exquisitely beautiful in the richness of the design and taste of this fruit?

Be of good cheer, and melt into the day's choices and opportunities. Much can and will be accomplished. You are not alone; angels stand with you right and left to assist you. No more being small—you would really rather be BIG anyway. Align with the Mighty and go forth.

So it is.

Archangel Gabriel

I am embarrassed to say I did not do as I was told and sat on these messages for many years. I want to encourage everyone to speak their truth and be their True Selves by expressing their unique gifts in the world. This is our purpose and our legacy at this time of our lives. I wish I had dared to publish this book many years ago.

The surprises kept coming in the following message, which felt quite personal. I received it from an angel who identified as Joyel. I had trouble accepting that I might receive a message from an angel that was not familiar to me and that I had never heard of. But after feeling the energy of this angel, I chose to accept him as one of my team of guardian angels.

A Personal Message from Angel Joyel

Good day,

It's a good day to walk in oneness energy. It's a GREAT day to align with cosmic beings. All is available in the Akashic records for assimilation in the spirit of oneness.

Taste the joy of this. It is your divine right and gift to do so. Do not doubt that life loves you. All your angels applaud the growth and opening of your energy field like a flower in spring. Be nourished by the breath of love that is an ocean around you that holds all within its flow.

Begin to exercise the muscles of the light body within. Do not second guess. Do not try too hard. Relax—it is fun, is it not? See, the connection is here as it always has been, but now it is easier and easier to tap into.

Walk in this power today and always. It is not hard, but natural and a part of you. Be joyous in the ability to stand with Heaven, to talk with angels, and to translate vibration into words of direction and encouragement. We stand with you.

I stand over you to help with this facilitation, for **I AM MIGHTY in the strength of love**.

(I ask if this being has a name.)

My name is ancient and written in symbols of fire and the Holy Spirit. For reference, you can call me Joyel of the purple ray of compassion, combining the blue and red, for cutting through with the strength of the sword of Michael the Archangel, the pink of love, and the power of the ruby ray. This is a powerful combination, and that is why I say, "I AM Mighty."

(I think that maybe this Joyel was the angel who came in my first message saying, "I AM Mighty." I continue to wonder about it all.)

You are not allowed to feel powerless and small anymore! For I stand with you, and my wings are tipped in electric gold like the sunrise.

It is indeed a new day—arise in this day. No fear! It is not a day to be holding back or playing small. The heavens are opened, and the Earth rises to meet with it. Feel the energy coming from above and below.

And so it is. Amen.

Joyel

Note: The purple ray represents mercy and transformation. In an article by Whitney Hopler, titled "Angel Colors: The Purple Light Ray, Led by Archangel Zadkiel," it is stated that "Purple ray angels may also come on missions to deliver peace and joy to you when you've successfully made changes God has called you to make" (www.learnreligions.com).

It finally occurred to me that I should ask my guides and angels questions: What should I do with the messages that come through? As I sat down to write, my inner question was: "How can I serve humanity?" I received the following answer.

How Can I Serve?

Continue to make daily connections—daily practice. Write more—you know it calls to you. Give up excuses—just do it! There are spaces. Learn to connect with spirit quickly and in many ways and places.

You know it is a matter of focus. You've done well at clearing your mind, as the illusions of daily drama have very little allure anymore. You could say that you've done it all—at least enough to know it is a sham, a dead end, like ashes in the mouth.

Maintain focus and pay attention. You will feel the answers more and more in your system.

Be happy, let loose, and enjoy the life you live. It is blessed, and your advantages are many.

As you call in the fullness of who you are, you will gain more clarity. Relax and allow. Do not judge the answers you receive. Let the mind rest and quiet. The protective personality is standing "at ease."

There is so much potential for expansion here. Continue to follow what speaks to you.

BOLD is a good word. Step into the larger version of Self.

Channeling will serve your spiritual path and allow your vibration to rise higher. You need not seek. All is within and will unfold in the proper order. Do not concern yourself. Trust the process. You know all this.

Do what seems fun to you. It is your life to create. Realize the best version of Self. Be centered and grounded—aware of the tuning fork within. Resonance is your focus and vibration is your expertise.

Write, write—the flow is backing up and begs to be released—you feel the pressure. Even if it does not seem relevant, it is not your job to censor this. Do not slow down to analyze what is coming—your job is to allow the flow.

Edit later if you must. Do not let the mind dictate or stand in the middle. Practice setting it aside and just allowing the words to accumulate on the page. Be surprised with the message—be delighted with what is to be a revelation to you.

"ALL THAT IS" seeks expansion—the leading edge—the unknown of what else, what more? This is not the function of the mind but only of Spirit. The physical world of the third dimension is being left behind. The next steps are unknown. You have been groomed for change, resilience, and the coming shift. Play the part that you wrote within yourself. It is very colorful—just the way that you like it.

Be easy. All is in order. You will find as you just flow and do not question what is happening, that the next step appears under your feet. Follow the "yellow brick road"—the crystal city awaits your discovery. (The angels like to use these metaphorical images to relate ideas to me.)

Celebrate the victory of the Earth's ascension and the growing tide of the wave of love that is upon you—upon all.

Float—surf—enjoy the Sun on your face.

Be in the moment. All is provided as promised—always.

We LOVE you mightily!!

The Angels

Writing these first messages gave me, and perhaps you too, the basis for understanding what follows as they become more universal and applicable to a larger audience. I had to set my mind aside to write the messages and let my hand move the pencil on the paper. Sometimes, moving at great speed would cramp my fingers. The words formed on the page, and I did not edit them because the coded transmission that comes with them forms between the lines and in the spaces.

It is my belief that there is only one of us here. We are created as the expressions of the mind of God/Source/the Creator, and what applies to one applies to all. So, I offer these transmissions, light packets of angel energy, as messages to you and the world.

I encourage you to find what resonates with you and is helpful and uplifting in these messages and to leave the rest. Although there is information and support for the whole world, we are still unique individuals with our own guides and free-will choices to make.

Our job is to follow our joy—to find what touches us at the core of our being. Each one of us has sacred one-on-one enlightenment and transformation to attend to.

At the end of each chapter, I offer a tool that you can use to become more in tune with your angel guides. Realize that they are a part of your wholeness, and guidance comes from parts of yourself that you are not in touch with yet. You are building the communication bridge to higher frequencies that are part of your subtle bodies, with which you will have an intimate relationship as you awaken to them.

2

MESSAGES FOR THE WORLD

I t is important to me that the messages received from other realms help others. I am basically lazy, and if I "have to" go through this process of awakening, expansion, transformation, and embodiment, I want it to be for a larger purpose. I requested that the messages be not just for me but also answers for the world at large, or at least "my tribe" of followers and family members.

One thing they are emphatic about is that they want us all to know that if you ask, there will be answers. They want you to know that the world needs you and me—we are each needed. The Angels want the world to know that all creation is a manifestation of God's love, always, forever as stated in the following messages.

Ask, and It Is Given

*The Angels **ARE always here**, so call on us. The action on your part sets an intention and vibrational connection that must be answered. It is the*

ASK = GIVEN phenomenon. You see, it is a complete equation. What would you ask, oh, people of Earth?

The cry goes up for completion, for wholeness—and yet you ARE whole. Do you not feel it? Love surrounds you at every turn. The love of God—of hosts of heavenly beings. It is a miracle and yet commonplace—the norm, so to speak.

Turn your radio dial and frequency to receiving. Be the receiver. Raise your frequency!

*Quiet the mind that carries your energy away to things that do not matter. Refocus in every moment to what does matter. If wholeness is that for you now, imagine wholeness—connect to that holiness and **BE** it!*

Ask yourself as that wholeness, what does it feel like in your body? A rush of energy, a tingle in the wiring of the cells? Keep your focus there. Ask Christ Consciousness to boost it even more. Intend that your body holds this light, this feeling, the love and compassion. Understand?

All this is available NOW for the asking, in this moment of NOW. For that is where everything is present. The ALL THAT IS. Simple and yet true.

What does wholeness feel like? A fullness? Fill yourself up with the fullness of it. Is it JOY? Ask for that. Allow yourself to feel that. Again, be electrified with the infusion of joy. Feel it in your energy centers, spinning with happiness.

See? It is already within your power.

It is not something that requires you to climb Mount Everest in the snows of winter, is it? Why do you make it so hard? No, do not look for justification. Do not allow the mind to go down that path and fall into THAT HOLE once again. But only know it is easy.

It only takes practice—like riding a bike. Practice.

Ask yourself, what do you really want and why? Follow down the string of whys until you discover that it is happiness and love that you are truly after underneath all the wanting. Do not settle for substitutes—for lifeless things will never satisfy.

Go for the GOLD! It is within reach, for it is who you are.

What does that mean? It means that as you nourish yourself and your body, it will find that wholeness within. It wants to be whole; it yearns to be whole, and it is the power within you that drives you forward.

Wholeness is consciousness and awakening to that connection with Source—a bonfire of energy greater than the Sun.

I AM MIGHTY, and I stand with you! *Be not afraid. All you want is yours. Receive it! Allow yourself to open to it. It is easy and natural. Ignore the mind that does not "get it"—that does not feel it rising within you, for it will sabotage you yet again if you allow it.*

Allow yourself to be lifted up—to fly above the radar of what the mind knows—into the great beyond of PEACE, LOVE, JOY, and follow THAT rainbow HOME.

Do it NOW!

And so it is. AmeN.

The Angels

It was curious that sometimes the messages conclude with AmeN with the capital "N" at the end. Isn't that interesting? The messages seem to have different voices. There seem to be distinct individuals or frequencies. As I work with them, I become more attuned to the energies of the messages, and which Archangel is likely to step forward with a blessing.

I love the imagery they often use to punctuate the message. For example, "Follow THAT rainbow HOME." What joyous imagery that is!

I can feel that the angels are so joyful to be heard and give instructions on connecting with them in the following message.

The World Needs You

Good evening,

It is good to be here and good to be heard. The sound I emanate is a vibration of light, weaving patterns of geometric construction in third-dimensional God-manifested reality.

To gain clear messages, it is necessary to clear the mind of your own thoughts. Clear any preconceptions of what is to come—of what Spirit wishes to say. For Spirit is not the same as conscious thoughts or of consciousness.

Consciousness must rise within you and be moved to the forefront of the body, and the desire to be one with Source. It can move one forward to come to an understanding—a knowing of the truth of the awakening with and without.

The love which we are flows ever through you to the Earth and all thereon— the love of Spirit for you is infinite and forever. Wrap yourself in the embrace of that love, and don't let go. The world needs you and your connection to the energy that flows to the world at this time of the great victory, of love, and the joy of creation.

I AM THAT I AM, and I AM mightily in love with you and with all. *This will resonate and sing in the particles of the cells, the* *air, the spaces between the spaces. It is beyond comprehension, so just accept and bathe in this happiness that flows like a river of gold—of thick and silky substance pouring in to stick to you like tar. Like that tar baby of the old Brer Rabbit children's story.* (I hear laughter.)

It (love) *is stuck to you as richness, whether you want it or not. For the time of waiting is over, and the blessings of Heaven pour out to overflowing in celebration that **love has won** and will win the day, in the ever-present NOW.* (Again, there is laughter.)

And so it is. AmeN.

The Angels

For those who don't know the story of Brer Rabbit and the Tar Baby, you might enjoy reading it. It is excellent for a laugh! My angels laugh, do yours? Personally, I am a serious person, so they are always telling me to have more fun and to lighten up—so far, I have not complied.

Heavenly messengers want us to know that everything is love. The world and everything it entails are just a reflection of that greater love. This message reminds me that God also loves our world. I believe our "Mother Earth" is a sentient being of immense power in her own right.

The World Is a Reflection of God's Love

The world in all its glory is just the reflection of God's love. Although the beauty of it can make you weep and the thought of leaving it behind breaks your heart, the magnificence of merging with oneness is even more overwhelming.

*The love that flows through everything—the real light—is like the difference between the Moon and the Sun. The Moon only reflects the Sun's light. One can hardly look at the glory of the light of the creative Source. It would seem to explode your very being. Can you imagine such a feeling of being enveloped in this? It will break your heart wide open to find and feel the grandeur of **ALL THAT IS**—the great **I AM**.*

*Yes, it is no small thing to raise your frequency in gratitude, in compassion, in the love of God/Source. But there is more, and once you have a taste of "going home" to that love—that love that, in fact, you truly are—you will know that this is the **only** thing that is real.*

It seems a shame to label this beauty of Earth life to be a dream, an illusion, a hologram, but once the joy of the discovery of light, love, energy, and eternal bliss grabs your attention and finally takes you over, you will see clearly.

Beloved, love the life and the experiences that being "God in action" brings you. Weep not for those who do not see it as you do—those who cannot feel the miracles, for each soul is unique. Each person is a unique part of the whole, and each will reflect the light a little differently. That is how it should be. Each frequency of God is required for the grand symphony.

Allow the music to play on in all its variations, to come to a crescendo in the perfect chord of unity and complete oneness. It can be no other way, after all.

Be at peace and know that I AM GOD, and each of you can never be anything other than that completion of oneness.

And so it is.

The Angels

For those who want to communicate with angels, prayer is a tried-and-true way of tuning into spirit. It is a great place to begin. To tune into spiritual energies, we bring our energetic patterns into harmony and resonance with them. They said that words don't particularly matter except in the context of your belief in what you are saying. The purity of heart and intention will put you in touch with angels and your highest version of self.

Tool #1 – Prayer: Example for Divine Guidance and Mercy

"Beloved, I AM Presence. I call in the presence of angels and archangels as my spirit guides for continued guidance and mercy in everything I say and do. Make me an instrument of thy peace to move with love in the world, and may my efforts be enough. Let me always be grateful and allow joy to rise within me. Amen."

Experiment with different prayers that make sense to you and then practice listening for an answer. Asking does create an answer; even more to this point, in quantum science, the answer is contained in the question—it is a complete formula.

Write a prayer or two that resonates for you here as a reference.

_____

_____

_____

_____

_____

_____

3
BIG CHANGES ARE HAPPENING

*W*hen I began writing messages, I was often awakened in the middle of the night between 3:00 a.m. and 5:00 a.m., knowing that the angels had something they wanted to say. I write mostly at night when it is quiet, and I am not distracted by anything from the outside world. It is easier to focus and relax my mind, which is still doubting what is happening.

I am uncertain why I'm writing this all down, but I do it anyway. I collect my writing in many notebooks, but don't share any of it—it still seems pretty crazy.

The messages in this chapter seem personal, yet also apply to all of us who are awakening now due to energy shifting. After some years, I discovered that many people are connecting to their guides and guardian angels.

I imagine you are one of these people who already know angels because you are interested in reading this book. Perhaps you have been doing it all your life, and it's not new to you.

Many of the messages here are about change and navigating it—the personal, family, and larger-world changes that are part of our life story and addressed by the light beings I call angels. Most of my messages are from the Archangels and sometimes the larger group of angels, but over the years, there have been messages from Ascended Masters and other guides calling themselves the Counsel of Light.

Humans do not like all the change. We try really hard to maintain the status quo and keep life running along familiar paths. Unfortunately, without friction, there is no growth, and growth requires more change. Angels can help us adjust to change. I propose that we will not make it through the coming changes with ease and grace without divine help and guidance from our spiritual guides of light and love.

Premonitions of Unsettling Change

Be awakened by the energy. Arise and listen, for there is much of note happening on other levels.

The shift is gaining momentum, and the call of the hour is to stay the course. Ride the wave. It is unsettling to all creatures. There is a restlessness that has no logical explanation—a smoke on the wind, a premonition that things are about to change. Something is happening.

Though all are feeling the effects of change, the reactions are varied and unsettling for all. You are in an unknown energy—the other side of an 11-11 portal of change. A place in the space-time continuum that the Earth has not been in before. It is of galactic proportions.

The dimensions of even the higher realms do not even have the same physics that has been known in the past. There is no way to keep up with it all without surrender—without letting go of trying to keep control and trusting. Let go! Hanging on at all will not serve you.

The challenge is one of letting go and still finding your balance on the surfboard of life. You were born for this. You have prepared for eons. All will unfold in divine order, which, though strange, makes perfect sense from the higher perspective.

(In this message, I see a visualization and a picture in my mind's eye. This visual message is like a packet of energy—a complete message that is being downloaded. It is like a story unfolding. This is something new to me and a quite interesting twist to just having the words flow in.)

Do not concern yourself with what others are doing. You see them streaking by like passengers on the southbound subway train while you are in the one going north. Your destination and timelines will cross but still run separately.

Do not forget those who ARE on the same subway car—the same train, the same train track—going through the underground tunnel with you. The destination approaches. You are on the right route for you. You have the ticket. Remember?

Surfboards, trains, tunnels, and bus stops—all are metaphorical to orient you to a new way of traveling through time. Although time and space are collapsing, some things that are familiar will remain in your dreamscape.

As the signposts in your life seem less familiar, you need not worry. Comfort those who also feel the disorientation. Pass around many hugs, warm blankets of compassion, and hot drinks of comfort to those who experience the changes in a traumatic way.

Many find themselves without anchors, like those devastated in fires and floods that strip them of all they once knew. Pray for them. Hold them in your heart with compassion.

There is "a tremor in the Force, Luke," to quote the movie Star Wars.

(All this is what I am seeing and hearing. The images and impressions keep coming.)

Clear the decks! We are through the portal of the 11-11 gateway, like it or not. That signpost has come and gone and is behind you now in the journey—the linear journey of this time-space reality.

Reach for the multidimensional perspectives. See with the inner sight, and feel your way. Your soul knows the way. Your Higher Self holds the tiller, and Source has set the sails.

(I think, "And now a sailboat metaphor? Really?")

How about a little smile, beloved? Try not to take it all so seriously.

Although this is the part of the hero's journey where there is doubt and the waves are choppy, the vessel does make its way through the narrow passage and weathers the storm. That is in the script and the preview of the turning cycles.

Center yourself in your core energy. Breathe through the emotional anxiety. Eat right. Get enough rest and be diligent in your self-care, including your daily sacred practice and meditation. Those rituals will sustain you through this time.

Continue to organize and declutter or the winds of change will do it for you. Let go of the old ways of being. It is hard for you, we know. You have our love, comfort, and support. We applaud your courage in this undertaking. All of this galaxy and beyond are cheering you on to the victory that belongs to all as one.

It is not too far off that the reward of oneness will shimmer into view like a mirage in the desert and solidify out of the ethers. You will see.

Be steadfast in your faith, trust, and desire to serve and to love.

All is well.

And so it is.

The Angels

I still sometimes struggle to follow the angels' advice. Why is it so hard to do as they have guided and instructed? We know better, but what do we do? I am often reminded to practice what direction I have graciously been given. We are tasked with seeing things from a completely different perspective than we are used to. There is a quantum shift that will be the transformation that we are seeking. It takes being more conscious of the energy. Here is what the angels say:

Stepping into Unknown Change and Challenge

Stepping into the unknown is a challenge, but one that you are ready to meet. The challenge of turning your world inside out from third-dimensional format to fifth-dimensional reality is no small task. It requires conscious dedication, surrender, and trust in the divine plan and support that Heaven offers you.

These blocks are ones that dissolve as the ego finds its right use in your multidimensional frequency. Do not fear! All is unfolding as it should. Relax and be present with each magical moment of your unfoldment like the butterfly during its metamorphosis, and as the spark of light becoming a conscious electromagnetic being of that light that is also an alchemical transformation.

Do you trust the Universe? Check in with yourself whenever you notice the tightening of resistance to what his happening in the body.

Breathe in and direct the light/love/intention into that feeling in the physical body. It will dissolve in energetic coherence with the divine love that you are allowing into your life.

It's about the embodiment of that love and that light. You must allow your power as that light being to shine forth. You are so much more than you ever imagined.

Say yes to all that wants to be released to make room for the new template of humanity that is awakening and coming online. The old ways want to go. They come up to be released. See them as the old energies of the past. Become new!

Be that bright light that truly you already are! Behind the iron mask of illusion is the real king—the real queen of the realm.

Smile, step forward as royalty, and greet all who are cheering for you. Take your bows. Claim your many victories won! Enlightenment has come. The wave of fifth-dimensional love energy is cresting.

And so it is.

The Angels

As I read these messages at the time of publication, I am honestly embarrassed by my snail's pace and the disbelief that has held me back. It has been a process, and the angels ask us to give ourselves grace and be gentle with ourselves. We take one step at a time and enjoy the experience of the unfolding patterns.

Cosmic Winds of Change

It is such an exciting time, and the awareness of this is all around you. Be blessed by the winds—the cosmic winds of change—as the Earth moves into a "space" that it has never been in before.

The sacredness of each day and moment of this journey is not lost because of lack of mental awareness. It happens on a finer frequency than the mind perceives. But soon you will be able to connect the dots.

(I find that my hand is moving of its own accord, drawing dots, and then connecting lines on the page. This is different and weird.)

The lightworkers of Earth, of which you are a part, are moving forward collectively on all levels. You are not, and have never been, alone. Rest in that knowingness. All are one, you know. The doors of Heaven open and pour out the blessings that have been held for you—for all—for so long.

Although time is not real, the factoring of its rule in the physical world still remains in the dimension where you have found yourself. Linear thought has its purpose. Do not fight with it! Flow, flow—it is a downhill ride.

The oracle cards and your intuitions are not mistaken. The messages you get are real.

(I must have had this question in my mind at the time. I love to play with oracle cards and often get guidance and reassurance there to help me navigate the day.)

As those who pass from the screen of life on Earth are demonstrating for you, the body has to integrate and catch up to what already is. And this is a collective growth, an evolution, a revolution of consciousness—the like of which has not been seen before. It is great to be on the leading edge.

Do not resist, beloved. Do not get hung up with appearances—you can and will move the awareness and perception forward. Keep the faith. Do not falter. The angels support you—the collective supports you. You cannot fail. As they say, "Love has already won." Be happy in that knowing.

Sail the seven seas of the cosmic winds. Lift the sails of your heart's wings and soar. There is a reason you love flying and all manner of wings. Like the science fiction movie Close Encounters of the Third Kind, *you cannot keep from noticing the designs and signs of the place that calls you—the destiny that sings to you.*

It is a crazy compulsion, isn't it? The desire to know more is pulling you— pushing you—drawing you like a leaf on the breeze, then pushed by the wind that arrives before the storm.

The electricity of the storm of nature—of nature's forces—crackles with a charge of excitement. Let it come as it will. You will stand. You know how to push your roots deep into the energy of the Earth—the bedrock that holds you like the oak tree. The stronger the wind, the more the roots can, and do, go down.

Breathe, drink water, move your body. You can feel the circuits connecting those dots within and without. Be of good cheer. You do not need to know how it all works out, for "it is a mystery" until it isn't. Rest in that.

Continue to do your daily work and dance the dance of the leaf. Sing the song of the birds that know it is spring and time for cycles to turn. You are a part of all of it.

All of it IS You!

And so it is.

(At this time, I received a download of energy through me that burned all over like fire in my nerve endings.)

So HAVE THAT! Do you feel that? The electric heat flowing through? Don't forget to breathe. Feel the burn. It is okay. The new DNA is coming online (in my awareness, I sense the sound of laughter) *or the "old" DNA of the lineage of the starseed within. The heat of it feels good.*

Ready or not, the power that is you will come online. It can be a little spooky but more like magical, mystical, and even holy if you will allow that feeling to be dominant.

It is alright, little one—be soothed by the larger presence. You know how good it feels, even if it is somewhat confusing.

The Grace has come.

Come HOME.

The Angels

(The angels draw a heart as their signature and conclusion this time. I am crying, weeping with joy at the idea of the heavenly HOME.)

All that talk of massive changes is disquieting and is not angels' usual love and light messages. Some of this seems strange and weird. What could they be talking about, I wonder?

In retrospect, these messages make more sense after all we have been through in the past few years, with the pandemic and how our lives have changed drastically worldwide. Now, I find comfort in knowing that the angels were trying to prepare us for what was coming. I wish that I had been brave enough to publish their words earlier.

I apologize for my fear, uncertainty, and all of my shadows that were active in not acting sooner. I still struggle with the idea of being seen as a crazy angel lady in our world, even though there is more talk of angels all the time.

Tool #2 - Affirmations Exercise

I offer these affirmations to help us call on the angels, allowing us to go with the flow, have faith and trust in the divine plan, and make changes with ease and grace.

- "I trust in the divine plan and welcome change as a pathway to my highest good, guided by the loving presence of the angels."

- "With Archangel Michael by my side, I stand strong in faith and courage, embracing change as a divine opportunity for growth and transformation."

- "With Archangel Zadkiel and the Violet Flame, I release the past and embrace forgiveness of the past with grace and ease."

- "I am open to the new opportunities that change brings, knowing that my guardian angels support and uplift me every step of the way."

- "Through divine love and wisdom, I surrender, allowing the angels to lead me to greater freedom and joy."

You can make anything you wish for into a positive, affirming statement that anchors its energy in your mind, body, and spirit as a reality. As you repeat these things, brain circuitry comes online, turning it into belief over time. What you believe you can achieve.

Write your affirmations here for easy reading when you need them.

_____

_____

_____

_____

_____

_____

_____

_____

_____

_____

_____

_____

_____

_____

_____

_____

_____

_____

_____

_____

_____

_____

4

LOVE IS THE ANSWER

s I have received many messages over the years, the immense love of the angels is always present. When people ask me what they, the angels, are talking about, I always say they speak of love. They say that love is the universal solvent and the creative glue that binds everything together. They are proof that love is forever.

During this time, my dear youngest sister was suddenly diagnosed with cancer and shortly after transitioned from this life. It was a massive loss to me and my family. Christine was the glue, the one who organized our get-togethers and hosted family events. She is greatly missed.

Massive changes and upheaval have continued in the world around us, and we all feel the loss of no longer relevant ways of life. These messages are still relevant and fresh in this atmosphere of chaos and change. It is my belief that Love binds us together through all dimensions of time and space and through eternity.

Looking back on these early messages, I am shocked at the changes we have been through! We know that change is always constant, and we are being asked to step into the unknown and face our feelings and deep subconscious fears.

The angels want us to know that love is the answer, no matter the problem. The love we all seek is Christ Consciousness, personified for us in Jesus Christ, Buddha, and others. Consciousness and love expand, and love is often used as a synonym for life. Life is tough and very complex sometimes, and relationships may break our hearts; the angels admonish us to "see only love."

Never Fear—Only Love

Love is all there is—there is no death. We/you exist in the mind of God, which we are—where all is one and all is God.

That fullness of love beckons you on to complete the marathon of the ages, to bring humanity to the evolution of consciousness—the oneness we/YOU desire so much.

Mankind will know the God within each one of you as the energy rolls through—as time passes.

Your job is to leave some footprints to follow. Know that each person has their role to play and plays their part in the great story of the ages.

Be of good cheer, for the awakening once begun will gain momentum to create critical mass. So many things will change. Live in that vision of the New Earth. Yes, ground yourself there. The joy of oneness will lift you up—remember the feeling, connect to that frequency.

See the sparkling jewels of the gifts of Heaven that pour in. They are so glorious! Let all celebrate the coming of the light!

Know that the angels hear the wishes of your heart. Oh, the expanded heart— the secret chamber that breaks open with compassion and calls for mercy in these last days.

It is good to see the expanded worldview—even the galactic view—and be upheld with understanding of the importance of every thought, word, and deed. Enjoy the victory! Cheer on the players and your team! All are one.

Offer comfort to those who mourn with the assurance that all is in order. The plan moves forward, and each soul has free will to construct life and death on their own terms. There are no wrong choices.

Ultimately, love and unity consciousness is the outcome for the immersion in ascension's flame.

I say again—be of good cheer! Understanding and knowing will come. Each day there is progress. Never fear—only love.

Allow and Awaken!

The sleeping giant of your Higher Self is awakening. You are enormous, even more gigantic than you can ever imagine.

Do your best and carry on.

And so it is.

The Angels

As hard as it is to have compassion for others, the biggest challenge seems to be loving and accepting love for ourselves. We are often our greatest critics and hold ourselves accountable for the troubles of the world. We wish for love, peace, and brotherhood of men, yet we become confused about how to make it happen.

In this message, they let us know that the key is in loving ourselves and letting in the love that Heaven holds for us and wants to bless us with.

Love and Compassion for All, Including Yourself

It is good to come together in groups of Christ-conscious individuals to reflect on the God in all. The energy created is more than the sum and is multiplied.

The feeling of irritation can be chewed on as the moving parts of the energy fields. The vibrational dissonance is then changed to oneness by the universal solvent of love.

There is then acceptance of one another as you accept yourself as the beautiful, unique creature that you are—a pattern of God. You are a light shining in the wilderness. And yes, we are all also walking each other home at the same time.

There is no need to fear another, beloved, because it is only yourself that you meet along the way. Just say BOO and laugh. (I hear the laughing of Spirit.) *BOO!*

Are you so scary? There is only one of us here. Is God so scary to you? NO. Well then, surrender the fear and see only God in others—for in truth, love is all there is. Say that again—LOVE IS ALL THERE IS.

Feel into it—feel into the spaces and see the face of God there. It's good to feel the vibration speed up. It is good to visualize the things around you as only energy.

Circulate the energy as a vortex of divine love and compassion that transmutes all it touches—the tornado that lifts up all the trash and carries it away—the great wind of cosmic purpose. You start the spin and see what happens.

Set your intentions and allow Source to bring it home to you. You need not go anywhere. What you want is traveling toward you.

You frown because the world will not come up to speed to make it easier to sustain your spin. Beloved, what fun is that? How can you show the power and force of the mighty vortex of light that you are? You really don't like things to be too easy, do you?

So rejoice in the opportunities that arise daily, and act in accordance with love and compassion for all, including yourself. It is the measure that you meet out to the world.

Make it BIG and MIGHTY—this love that you are, that we are.

This is the fullness of GOD—the embodiment of Source.

AmeN.

The Angels

The angels addressed humanity's fears, which cause separation and are the source of much of our suffering. They give us hope and encouragement to find and be the love that we are made of.

Next, they speak about our division and the conflict in the world. They introduce the concept that we are only fighting within ourselves, the microcosm and the macrocosm, which reflect the same repeating patterns. They champion unconditional love and open the door to forgiving others as we forgive ourselves.

Support and Love Others Still Unconscious

The urge to cut off your love and support from those who choose to remain in lower densities of reality is understandable. It is difficult to comprehend why others choose to remain in darkness and suffering.

You understand that there is a choice—you have the power to choose and the help of angels. There are those who are so entangled in the illusion that they feel there are no choices. They need your love more than ever. They cannot see.

This does not mean you need to join them in their darkness, but only to view them with compassion. See them as the divine wholeness that they really are, and know that they will get tired of the density and reach for the light.

Shine a light for them. Be a light in their lives. Do not abandon them in their darkest hour. The darkest hour is just before the dawn.

Pain is often the path to awakening. All must awaken in their own time and in their own way. You cannot do it for them. You would not want to rob them of their victory after all, would you?

Trust in your divine plan, trust in the plan for all, and know the perfection of each life.

Love unconditionally each part of the whole—each spark of the oneness of creation. All fits in the infinite consciousness of the Great I AM.

Do not abandon the parts of yourself that need more love to break free of density that just needs to step up in vibration. Each cell, each soul just needs a shift in frequency to shake off the illusion of separation and come into the Christ consciousness of love.

Remember that the answer is more love—not less. More compassion, more mercy, more . . . . There is so much more. Let it in! Let it flow through! Let it lift all a little higher!

Sometimes, those you love the most seem unable to receive their wholeness. The resonance of the new energy is jarring, even shaking them violently like a rocket before liftoff. Be steadfast in holding space. Know that there is divine timing. All is well, even in the darkness.

And so it is.

The Angels

Tool #3 – Feel the Love Exercise: Hands Braided Over Heart

Purpose:

This hand gesture (mudra) promotes heart health, balances the heart chakra (Anahata), and cultivates feelings of love, compassion, and connection.

How to do it:

- Sit comfortably with your palms facing upwards on your thighs.
- Lace your fingers together in front of you
- Place your hands palms out over the center of your chest
- Hug yourself with the energy of love that flows between your hands and heart
- Close your eyes and take deep breaths.

Benefits:

- Strengthens the heart and regulates palpitations.
- Eases gastric issues.
- Reduces stress and anxiety.
- Promotes a sense of balance and calm.

Write about your experience of the energy in your heart, or draw a picture that represents this heartfelt experience.

_____

_____

_____

_____

_____

_____

_____

_____

_____

_____

_____

_____

_____

_____

_____

_____

_____

_____

5

ENCOURAGEMENT

*W*ith all the trauma we have experienced in life, in our personal lives and as a whole human collective, we need comfort and encouragement. We want to be held and soothed. We cry peace, peace—and there is no peace. There is no peace but the peace of faith, trust, and divine compassion.

The angels often say we are safe, we are blessed, and we are held in the arms of love. They are always here with words of encouragement to help us. And you will notice that they are often repetitive. Also, they do not follow the correct grammatical rules of speech. I have been careful to leave their wording in the messages despite what spellcheck wants to do to the manuscript.

Relax and Trust in Christ Consciousness

Peace. Peace be unto you—peace in your soul of souls. Begin to be steady and calm in knowing all is well. Life is unfolding as it should. You know this. Relax and trust.

There is nothing you need do but to follow the guidance of your soul. It knows the way home.

Home. Home is where the heart is. The flame within that burns unceasingly with love and light for The One is within you. The dream of life goes by and then all are reunited in love and light, in a place where in truth you never left.

Melt into the warmth of knowing, feeling, and sensing the realms of the cosmos that glow and shine, expand, and contract. Spin in the dance of The Divine. Oh, how beautiful! How perfect!

All creation sings in praise of the wonder of life and the infinite possibilities it affords all the creations of God.

All is in order—nothing and no one is lost—all are found. We hold you in the embrace of angels' wings. Brow to brow—third eyes locked in understanding and the peace of The One.

The Christ reigns again in the world. The course is set, and indeed love has already won. Rest in that knowledge and certainty. We sail toward the sunrise of a new day—on a New Earth—just as was promised of old.

The Christ is risen. You rise with the mist of Holy Spirit as it flows over the Earth.

Rest—Relax—Trust the flow!

And so it is.

The Angels

In a sound therapy tuning I received, the practitioner said that spirit wanted to know, "Now that you know that you have the power, what are you going to do with it?" I took this to mean this ability to know what the energy messages were saying, and the new powerful energies I felt.

In the following channeled message, I asked for more information on the subject of empowerment.

I want to point out to everyone reading this message that we all have the power of The Divine. We have just forgotten it. That is why we are currently experiencing an awakening. Many of us are feeling lost, disoriented, depressed, and alone.

The angels want to assure us that we are more powerful than we know. We have infinite possibilities in the infinite field of consciousness. We can and will connect to our Higher Self. We are ONE. It is our limiting thoughts and beliefs about ourselves that keep us living small. As we awaken, we are coming into our power as co-creators with the energy of vibrational frequencies of light; we manifest our reality and move into it.

What to Do with the Power

One of the issues facing you and all humanity is the limitations you put upon yourselves—the lack of imagination. There are truly no limits, only your comfort zone and possibilities. What can be done and what will be done is beyond your imagination at this time.

Never fear as you enter the space of the unknown—take each step that is in front of you with joy. That is the "mission impossible" of this time. It is the grandest adventure!

You are only just perceiving the beginning of the wave that will swell and take you with it in power and glory. Just float on the water. Find your balance on the surfing board and stand tall. All the rest is in the cresting of the wave. Ride 'em, cowboy!

(I feel my mouth going into a huge smile.)

Woo-hoo, and throw one hand in the air for a greater thrill.

(I envision riding a bucking bronco in some crazy rodeo show. Sometimes the guides and angels are so funny!)

Continue to surrender all the fears that do not serve you. Thank the people and experiences of the past that now float away on the sea of forgetfulness and lose their power over you. Face the shore and the dawn of a new day.

You have been told to ground yourself in the "New Earth" that is coming in. Indeed, this is good advice because Gaia is ascending to a more celestial frequency herself. She will no longer tolerate the pollution put upon her but will shake it off with or without humanity.

Thankfully, many people, especially in other countries and cultures more attuned to the Earth, are finding answers to help in the purification process. All that is needed will be forthcoming. Anchor there.

And so it is. AmeN.

The Angels

This message from years ago could be for me and maybe you today. I often feel that my dreams of peace on earth will never come true—at least not in my lifetime. The angels speak about the power of imagination, asking for help and believing so that we can anchor our larger version of ourselves into our physical bodies with joy. I don't know what this wonderful new age will look like for me, but they keep reminding us to envision our joy and to live life with faith and trust.

Envisioning Joy and Prosperity Is Key

Things will change more rapidly than you think. Imagine the best out-come in all situations, and believe truth, envision, and plan for that eventuality.

This is the year for action toward your goals as light workers. Do not hesi-tate or procrastinate the shifts that are necessary for the greater anchoring in of the light. Pray for the collective body of those who are the pledged leaders of this movement.

Each individual, everyone, is a piece of the great body of the work of the ages. The work is "easy" and the burden is "light," as an old hymn says. Still, it would benefit ALL if you would keep your eye on the prize of a New Earth.

The envisioning of the joy and prosperity of all is the key. Allow it to be true for you. Act as if it were true and all happens with perfect synchronicity.

The angels await your call. You can ask for blessings great and small—we only seek to assist you. All of your desires are worthy when the vibration is joy. Delight in the play of material manifestation—for it is your show, your story. What is the magical twist that saves the day?

You love that unexpected surprise do you not? The one that you did not foresee is the best. So just allow anything to be possible and unicorns to exist for you. You know what I mean.

Relax and let it all be true. Everything is unfolding perfectly—remember that. Collapse time if you need to, to allow for all to arrive safely home. That is the ending you prefer, is it not?

And so it is . . . so it is.

The Angels

I love the angels' encouragement and the interjection of magical, mystical options because I do believe in miracles. Do you?

In this following message, they talk about the "most beautiful symphony that all creation sings and reverberates with its sound vibration. It is enough to bring you to your knees in the ecstasy of its glory." The beauty of their words encourages and inspires me to continue with the challenges of life that offer more growth and eternal value in the larger perspectives that angels have in the celestial realms.

Learn to Live without Judgment of Others

What is relevant on Earth is the experience of living without judgment. Just observe life by registering the information of the senses. This information is energetic in nature and comes in as light/seeing, sound/hearing, smell/taste, and knowing/felt energy in the body.

Without the body temple, this information is not available, and that is why the human experience is so valuable in the mind of God. God is experiencing himself as God in all ways.

This may seem like a big experiment that has no heart, but I assure you there is nothing further from the truth. You could say it's ALL heart, in that everything is love—life manifesting. It is an awesome unfolding of the process of life.

The cycles turn—the spin is the most beautiful symphony that all of creation sings and reverberates with the sound vibration of it. It is enough to bring you to your knees in the ecstasy of its glory.

Do you not feel it in the wind on your skin and the song of the birds in spring? Listen to the laughter of the brook flowing to the sea and the waves on the shore. We could go on for pages about the reflection of God/Source everywhere, but it is your turn.

Look for that same expression of God in the eyes of every person—for it is the expression of you—God—Love that is the I AM. Is it not wonderful?

You are awakening to the joy that has always been within you. Let the blind see— let the Earth and all thereon be healed in the rising energy of consciousness and cosmic love. The councils of Heaven rejoice at the victory of the souls of Earth.

Celebrate all that you can perceive every day and breathe it into your senses. It will fill you up if you allow it.

Oh, dear ones, be of good cheer no matter what is appearing—you are eternally and dearly loved more than you will ever know. Receive that adoration now! Let it hold you and support you. Trust. Be present, and receive your blessings.

That is all.

The Angels

Tool #5 – Gratitude List

The value of gratitude and making a list is extraordinary! When I stop practicing gratitude, I wonder why I don't feel my best and must start again. We are responsible for keeping our vibes high to meet the angels halfway. This is easily accomplished by thinking of loved ones, and feeling gratitude is almost as high a vibration as love to strengthen your energy field.

- Every day, take the time to list five things that you are grateful for.
- Keep a journal; you can do this every morning or evening, but the idea is not to repeat the same things but to find five new things to be grateful for that day. You can do it!
- The more you look, the more you see; soon, you will have to hold some back to avoid filling a whole page at once.

List the first five "gratitudes" right now to start your practice and feel the expansive feeling of gratitude that vibrates with appreciation and love.

_____

_____

_____

_____

_____

_____

_____

_____

_____

_____

_____

_____

_____

_____

_____

_____

_____

_____

_____

_____

_____

_____

_____

_____

_____

_____

6

TOOLS FOR TRANSFORMATION

*S*ometimes, I believe that the angels are not quite in tune with the material world and the daily challenges we have to face. They do not experience the limitations that we do, and they do not feel the pain of our deep emotions.

The angels want to help us with everything but are bound by the Law of Free Will, and we must request help from them first. The law ensures that humans are free to create their experience on Earth as they wish. Everything is in accordance with our free will choice.

Still, the angels offer helpful tools to help us on our spiritual journey. Our experiences are what we take with us, and our love is what is everlasting from this Earth experience.

I notice, too, in the messages that angels seem to have a sense of humor and seem to laugh. I believe that they are giving us a sense of levity and raising our energy to a more receptive level for higher consciousness.

The Magic of Breath

Life is a magical gift, and each breath is a blessing. Isn't it amazing that each breath can connect you to Source? Who knew, right? (There is the sound of giggling.)

Well, the mind of God, which connects with you now, knows all things. All is eternally known and made of "God stuff." Why is this such a hard concept? Well, you set it all up that way—to experience everything separately that is, then bring that experiential information back into oneness. Expand and contract—inbreath and outbreath.

Every time you breathe, there is an energy exchange, and everything is forever becoming more—more conscious first of all, but this is also a paradox. How can there be more than all—the ALL THAT IS?

The mind cannot grasp it, so just feel into that and breathe some more. Relaxing into God is a great idea. Perhaps you could revisit that concept and the idea that there is nothing to do. Nothing is broken or wrong, and nothing needs to be fixed.

Stand in this knowing, and smile in the present. That is where God is, and that is where you will BE also.

Much love for you!

And so it is.

The Angels

One lesson I continue to learn is to do deep breathing daily to bring light energy into my body. It continues to amaze me how this breathing we take for granted is the gift of spirit and life energy itself. Yet we are so ignorant of this great blessing, and most of us breathe so shallowly that it is incredible that we don't pass out altogether.

The OM That Is Breathing You

The inbreath and outbreath of life, of consciousness, serves to nourish your soul. Like waves sounding on the beach and the chi of ocean energy, it renews you. Breathe in with the intention of nourishment. Breathe out with the release of stress and resistance to the presence of more light within you.

More and more light. How much will you hold? **You are a pillar, a temple, a tube of Source energy. Stand in your super-power. Take on the crystalline body that is tailored to fit only you.**

Try it on for size. Walk the Earth as the crystal light being that you are, and resonate with the ascension energy of the Earth body and the Sun.

Take the protective mutterings of your mind, and stick them in your pocket.

Feel into your cells and the spaces between that resonate with divine frequency. This is REAL! This energy is the pulse of LIFE and the breath of GOD.

Give yourself over to the great OM that is breathing you.

IT IS YOU!

OM

AUM

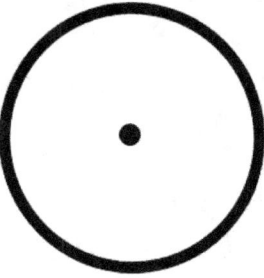

The Angels

I had an experience when I tried meditation for the first time. Suddenly, I was aware that I was being "breathed." It was as if my body was not in my control but breathing of its own accord. While the body does breathe without conscious thought, to be suddenly conscious of that happening was shocking and scared me for a moment. I quit with a start and felt that I had missed something significant.

The following is the first time a meditation came through from the archangels. It was in November 2018, and the 11-11 date was declared a portal of particularly potent light energy. This meditation has been published as an audio recording on my website and is often given as a free gift to all.

My daughter said that the meditation sounded quite ominous. I agree that it was not what I would expect an angel to reveal in a lovely meditation. Though I dare say none of us knows exactly how to judge what these divine energies called *archangels* are. Everyone who channels angels, archangels, and other spirit guides can only interpret the energy through their own lens, and you, dear reader, are urged to have discretion about what you choose to believe.

And now, after all the revelations about the pandemic and all that has happened since this meditation was given in 2018, I wonder why I did not understand the importance of the message at the time. Looking back, it was quite prophetic.

Gift of the 11–11 Portal Meditation: Archangel Michael

Change is imminent—Earth changes, political change, change in every area of life. The old energy falls away like crumbling sandstone. The foundations of one's life fall away, and what remains?

The core of all life is what is revealed—it is the God within. This truth has been covered with muck like the Golden Buddha that was hidden from invaders by a covering of plaster.

The "weather" of life's challenges has come to wash away all that is not needed anymore. The true worth and value of the soul—the fractal of God is the jewel that remains—that always remains. It is eternal.

Do you understand eternal? Not really—but you can feel into it.

(The meditation begins here. So, start with deep belly breathing.)

Breathe and fill up your lungs—center into your heart space with your breath. Shine the light of love and consciousness there, and feel it expand within you.

Now feel it move out, through the confines of the body into the spaces between the third-dimensional molecules of the material world.

Don't hold your breath. Breathe fully into that space as it flows into the OM of Earth's vibration.

Connect with the energy of the belly. The lower chakras there provide an anchor. Feel that anchor hold you in place, in the physical, as your radiance expands.

As it expands and the light energy pouring into you becomes a great pillar, crackling with energy, the upper chakras buzz with that increase of energy. Feel your crown chakra spinning and your whole cranial cavity fill until the ears vibrate with it.

You are a torch—a beacon—a lighthouse.

Breathe—breathe deeply, and take it in and through the cells of your body.

All distraction just flows through you and cannot distract or disrupt this force field.

The infinite is here. The eternal is here. You are the bridge between dimensions. You are Spirit incarnate—the light of the world.

Feel it in the center of your hands and the chakras there. Now feel the burning of those in the feet. Walk the Earth as an emissary of that light—that eternal flame.

Link hands with your angelic entourage, and go forth into your day.

Hold, breathe—hold this in your consciousness as an exercise. How long will you consciously hold it? Check in with the core of your being and all the energy centers, all day. Make this a daily practice.

Take your supporting beings of light with you. Say, "Archangel Michael, hold this energy in place within me. Surround me in your blue light with sparkling diamonds that cut through all dissonance and confusion—all darkness and stagnation."

Walk through the 11-11 portal of the new day as a symbol of the new cycles—new beginnings.

Begin again—and again. This is eternal—forever beginning, no ending, but a circle of love that binds us all in oneness.

And so it is.

Archangel Michael

Archangel Michael is one of the most well-known messengers of God. This meditation has been very comforting. Knowing that I can walk with angels and that they will hold my hand throughout the day to help has been a tremendous blessing. I want everyone to see the truth of this message. I have felt very close to Archangel Michael, and he is the Archangel who speaks with me the most. I am so grateful for his support and for continually bolstering my faith.

The Solution to All Problems: Vibrational Frequency

The best solutions to the problems you face daily are found in a different vibration than where those problems originated. You simply need a format change to see it.

You have heard what Einstein said: "You cannot solve our problems with the same level of thinking that created them." The question that arises for you to ask the angels is, "How do I get to a different level of thinking?" First, you must take your attention off the problem and release yourself from that stuck energy.

The heavenly host says to you, "Shift your attention to a place of gratitude, joy, happiness, love, etc.—then you can look again. The solution is right there." The solution is already connected to the situation energetically in the multiverse and can be easily accessed. It is so easy with an understanding of vibrational energy resonance and your freewill choice to become the master of your own frequency.

Once you familiarize yourself with the frequency of more enjoyable feelings—just go there. Practice this so you can direct the light of God through you into the physical.

The solutions magically appear as if written in invisible ink—right in front of you. The answer to your "hopeless situation" manifests easily. You will ask yourself, "Why did I not see this before?"

Of course, it works. It is only following a principle of quantum physics that seems magical in the third-dimensional world, where you have sat immobilized for too long.

Practice your "magic tricks"—the sleight of hand—make it a fun game. There are opportunities that you call problems that arise in your life daily to help you.

Soon, you are a "Master of the Alchemy of Spirit and Matter." You appear as the creator of energetic transformation wherever you go. Do not let it scare you, as it is beyond your current experience, but realize that the Master Jesus has given you many examples of this type of transmutation for a reason.

Jesus will tutor you when you ask. Ask him to elevate your frequency of love to the level needed for receiving the energy that he embodied. This will allow him to deliver teachings directly to you. Ask him what to do today to be more like him.

You can ask Jesus, Buddha, Elijah, angels, the Universe, or any and all beings of light to work with you. We love you and wish to assist you, but we cannot until the channel is open for receiving the transmission. Do you understand?

Open your mind with belief in what is possible. Don't you profess to believe that everything is possible for the Lord of All? Will you allow it to be true for YOU—in your life? Allow it!

If need be, practice forgiveness for your childlike misunderstandings. Forgive all that holds you back. The blocks that stand in your way are not evil but rather require a shift in understanding and frequency to move beyond them.

Release your old habits of blame and shame. Release the story of why—why it is the way it is.

The old energies do not serve your higher purpose or your destiny. Ideas that you have allowed to be laid upon you long ago, you have shouldered as a burden to carry forever more. The time has come for the great awakening.

Shake yourself all over like a horse does when the saddle has been removed after a long trail ride. Shake yourself like a dog after a bath or a swim in the river.

(The angels asked me and are asking you to please stand and shake. Do the shaking meditation of the masters of the East who know about the movement of the chi energy.)

Archangel Michael now draws his sword of light to cut you free and declares,

Stand up now. Shake up the cell memory in your body. Shake each part of you with movements you have never made before. This creates a new pattern within and without. Shiver and shake your physical body with the intention of waking up the molecules of the cells. Shake off the dust of decay and ancestral superstitions that have been encrusted around you. Reveal and awaken the light within! Are you shaking it up? Put on belly dancing music if you need to—but do it! Release, uncover, and reveal the answers, the solvent, and the solutions for everything that you want now. Everything you need is within you. Practice makes perfect.

And so it is.

The Angels

On this occasion, I jumped up and shook my body. You don't ignore angels when they tell you to do something. I was starting to get used to the interactions with the angels. The power of Archangel Michael was compelling, to say the least.

The "shaking meditation" that is mentioned here goes like this:

Stand with your feet spread and slightly bouncing to release the tension in your system. Swing your arms and move in a disjointed way, trying not to repeat the same movements but to repattern the brain by doing new combinations of giggling, swinging, jumping, rocking, and rolling your whole body and all its parts in such a way that allows the tissues and body to realign themselves.

As this subsequent transmission from the angels points out, part of asking for help is actively receiving the energy and blessing. In a previous chapter, we started the gratitude list, and now we learn how to receive these blessings that we are graced with.

Gratitude and the Miracle of Receiving

It's with a thankful heart that the soul awakens to itself. It is an act of fully receiving the life that you have been given. You have an abundance of opportunities to be grateful every day. This is wealth. Be full to overflowing with the grace and love of the heavenly hosts who always watch over you.

You can see the love that life holds for you if you only look for it. It will shine back at you through the eyes of all you meet. Meet all with joy and love. Meet them with compassion. Meet them in the depths of despair, for you will find God even there. Look and you will see. It is another complete equation—a magic formula like "ask and it is given."

The call goes out from your heart and is always answered by Spirit. Everything is for your benefit. Have trust in this, for it is the truth.

Gratitude for all that comes to you will only bring more to delight and surprise you. Be ready to receive all that Heaven's love wishes you to have. Your job is to make your receiving basket BIGGER—not to close down in fear and protection but open. Open the heart space!

If you do not know how, ASK! Ask the angels, "How do I open for the blessing that are coming to me?" Ask with expectation, curiosity, and desire for the answer. If you cling to your story of can't and won't, the river of blessing is shut off—squeezed off by your own free will. Understand? It's your choice.

Choose gratitude for small things, and great will be the reward.

Let it be a day of thanksgiving every day. You only have the ever-present NOW of consciousness to create your experience of life. Choose wisely!

Amen.

The Angels

On the day I channeled the following message, I asked the angels, "Should I wait on Spirit energy to move me, or do I go to Spirit and make a connection? Move or wait?" This is the answer that I received.

What Are We to Do?

Connecting and waiting on Spirit can both happen in the NOW moment, since now is all there is.

The opportunity is to make Spirit conscious in the third dimension—to take the Holy Spirit and anchor it on the Earth. All the chaos and information coming in at once can coexist in consciousness as awareness expands. When breathed into, it feels like fullness in the heart.

All those things "out there" that draw your attention from Source don't need to pull you off center. Hold your awareness in your core as the illusion flashes around you like a light show. It flashes like a movie in which you are no longer hypnotized by—lulled into unconsciousness by the story.

This is an interesting and new way to exist, isn't it? Sitting in loving presence and observing.

It feels somewhat like Neo in The Matrix *movie, moving in slow motion, looking at the bullets, and picking them out of the air. How is that—having awareness of what is coming and what is floating around you while centered?*

A FUN multidimensional experience, fully feeling that feeling. (Pause for an awareness of the feeling.) *Those things that require dealing with are no longer as irritating or disturbing to the peace within.*

Peace will not be disturbed. It is only "peace-full." What a concept!

What if you write as everything else goes on? How does that feel? The flow can go uninterrupted, as little energy is needed for the third-dimensional gnats that buzz around.

The amount of energy flowing is fast enough to move energy through the gunk that distorts all that is not love—it is pure consciousness. See the energy move, releasing any blocks as events show up.

Doing is not the answer—presence IS.

The Angels

I picture the visualization of the flow of energy as similar to the computer screen in the movie The Matrix, which is flowing with streams of information that look unintelligible but are being read by the technician. My new understanding is that we are the energy moving through us; it comes embedded in the breath and in the light, and both physical and cosmic waves are seen and unseen.

Thanksgiving and Gratitude for the Light Within

The joy fills the cells with each breath and fills the energy centers. It is calming and expansive at the same time.

Isn't it wonderful to be able to access this joy with focused awareness? It is truly always present when dropping the chatter of the mind that tends to distract from the allness of God presence which we are.

There is no greater joy than this connection with Source. Although this union is not what you thought or expected, the joy, bliss, and love are so profound—why wish for more? There is no more—this is the ALL THAT IS, the infinite one that you are and have been all along.

Yes, put your hands together in recognition, in gratitude, and thanksgiving over your heart. A true Namaste to you—to the infinite.

Although it is beyond understanding of the mind, the heart knows and will come online for full communion. It is available in the expanse of the timeless NOW. Just breathe—take a slow breath and FEEL it fill the spaces within and without.

You have made space within by your willingness to drop your karma, by your meditation that quiets the mind, and by your intention. You have made space by putting your attention on your body/breath and your experience of it.

While you believe you are still seeking, you have in fact found and been found. All you need is to rest in the arms of the cosmos.

This new consciousness of yourself as the evolving human is birthing within you. All else pales compared to this experience. Enjoy every day of this transition. Although it happens continually in the blooming of the universal mind, for you the ecstasy of the conscious experiential chemical feeling of joy is something uniquely human.

The whole of living cosmic energy rejoices with you—through you—at this place in time as you perceive it in your linear way of duality:

- *In and out,*
- *Inbreath and outbreath,*
- *In time and out of time.*

The celebration is profound; the light is within you, though the darkness "comprehended it not."*

It is not your concern, not your work, to contemplate what others are doing or the nature of their "darkness." Your work is only within your own experience and your own cells. Believe that all of life is in order—is loved and held in the arms of that Great Love. Let the worries of the world go. Release those you love into the care of the Lord of All.

This seems to you to be an efforting, even a war, conflict in duality. It is not so. The yin/yang is a complete whole. It is but a breath to GOD. A breath, I tell you! Easy. Allow yourself to know this—to feel this. Let all be in gladness at the grace of God and the mystery of it. Let the not-knowing within the mind be okay.

Enjoy your most sacred life. Walk as the light you are on the Earth plane. It is an experience that is only for YOU to have in the transmuting of the lower densities of matter within each cell, each level of the sacred geometry, and the unique vibration of YOU.

Let Heaven and angels sing. Let that song be heard and sung through you, as you, in the great chorus—the alleluia chorus.

Is this not WONDERFUL? Is this not the message you wish to carry, to anchor, to be? Of course, it is! Simply release your attention on all else.

See the larger picture. Turn your eyes, and include your inner eye. Focus with that inner eye, and turn away from the past. As Abraham-Hicks has said, "Look away! Just look away!" Take your vision from the old stories you have told yourself about life.

Now see yourself in slow motion—turn toward the light and **see only light and love***.*

And so it is.

The Angels

* From the King James version of the Bible: "And the light shineth in darkness; and the darkness comprehended it not" (John 1:5).

The angel messages include many references to meditation, and several of them are in this book. However, the angels don't discuss techniques or training. I did not start meditation until after my spiritual awakening. Then, I began a daily practice of 45 minutes of mantras and Om music. I want to return to that experience of Oneness, reach that wholeness, and feel total freedom of that state of being again.

I have since learned that there are so many ways to meditate to choose from; there is no excuse not to practice. It has become my most needed and appreciated spiritual support tool.

Tool #6 – Meditation Practice

Here's a short explanation of different easy meditation types. You can mix it up so you don't get bored, but start, even if it is only for 5 minutes daily. Your life will be so much better for it.

1. **Silent Meditation** – Sitting in stillness, focusing on the breath or simply observing thoughts without attachment. It promotes inner peace and clarity.

2. **Candle Flame Meditation** – Gazing at a flame (Trataka) to develop concentration and inner vision. This practice enhances focus and deepens meditation.

3. **Sound Meditation** – Using chanting, mantras, singing bowls, or Solfeggio frequencies to create a vibrational shift and promote relaxation.

4. **Walking Meditation** – Moving mindfully, focusing on each step and breath. It is ideal for those who struggle with sitting still, as it brings presence and grounding.

5. **Laughing Meditation** – Starts with forced laughter, which becomes genuine. Laughter releases stress, boosts joy, and raises energy.

6. **Breathwork Meditation** – Techniques like alternate nostril breathing (Nadi Shodhana) or deep diaphragmatic breathing regulate emotions and calm the mind.

7. **Dance or Movement Meditation** – Expressing energy through free movement (like ecstatic dance or Sufi whirling) allows emotional release and deep connection.

8. **Guided Visualization** – Listening to a narrator guide you through imagery for healing, manifestation, or relaxation.

Each style offers unique benefits, making it easy to find a meditation that resonates with your lifestyle! Which one interests you most? If you already meditate choose one that you have not tried to experiment with.

Write which one you choose and why.

_____

_____

_____

_____

_____

Mediate with angels and archangels in mind and what message they have for you. Write down what came through to you in meditation.

_____

_____

_____

_____

_____

_____

_____

_____

_____

_____

_____

_____

7
LIGHT/LOVE:
THE RESONANCE VIBRATION

*T*he angels often seem to use love and light interchange-ably. There is also some differentiation between love/light and light/love. I think this is because there are just not enough words to describe the types and kinds of love in English. There are phrases that editing programs would change as "incorrect" English. I have asked my editor not to change these things because I feel the way the angels have said things is part of the message, even though the difference is subtle. Words are energy codes, and the angels have said that the message is embedded within the energy between the words. This all sounds very mysterious to me.

Each angelic being's vibrational frequency is slightly different, and their energies are very subtle. I look forward to the day when we have telepathy and can understand many messages from cosmic sources without being deterred by language's limitations.

I have also noticed that angels repeat themselves with my message and other channels. This is not in error but in emphasis, and to take a moment to ponder what has just been transmitted. You may notice that in reading the messages as well.

Each Soul Must Shine Its Own Light

Each person is their own uniqueness. Your life story is your creation and has its own gift and message to give. Your spiritual path is unique to you and you alone. All are an individual divine spark burning with possibilities.

The individual soul's vibrational energy is the essence of a part of universal consciousness. It is priceless in its differentiation from all the rest.

Too much time and energy is spent by humanity to be like others—to be other than one's own true Self. You strive to belong by following the loudest voice. What a travesty! What a grave misunderstanding of one's life purpose. It is a form of darkness to cultivate sameness—it is an enslavement of the spirit.

Your children are taught to conform at every turn. Encourage their individuality, their brightness; what they bring to life, no one—NO ONE—can contribute but them. They're divinity incarnate.

The old way of controlling the mass consciousness is dying. It's breathing its last breath, and the death knell has been sounded. Let it die! Support curiosity and thinking outside the box, even radical new thinking. It is the evolutionary plan for humanity.

Be an example of joyously expressing YOURSELF—as you are—no filters. Be free in the fullness of love that you are. Express the divine creator within you. It gives others permission to explore what longs to be fulfilled within them. Creativity in all its outrageousness can be so beautiful when expressing love and joy from within.

It is only when love and divine expression are suppressed that today's teens act out in expressing the darkness and pain that they feel—even to taking their own lives and the lives of others. They have been blocked from their true mission. They have not been valued for their unique gifts. Help them explore and expand what begs to be revealed from within in loving-kindness. Their souls cry out for expression.

The new souls being born will be the leaders. Listen to them. Play with them. They come from a consciousness not yet manifested or recognized today. They must be allowed to blossom in the fullness of who they are—who they are here to be—in all their glory.

See the divinity in all. Begin with finding that divinity within yourself. You are not less than the brightest lights you see. You see the brightness of others BECAUSE you ARE that light.

Shine that light! Shine on bright star!

The Angels

Immersion in the Light

The waves of light and love continue to break upon the Earth body of Gaia and all thereon. The changes in the DNA structure roll forward, regardless that many are still unaware. Their day will come in this life or the next for immersion in the light.

The twin flames connect and are a blessing to mankind. The light workers are becoming masterful in their wielding of intention. Those who are awake cannot be unchanged, for they are forever changed in their focus and desires.

Continue to find your groups, your tribe, your band of brothers. Consciousness is finding unity in layers of awakened souls. The connectedness, the oneness, will continue in pairs, in groups, in tribes, in communities.

The truth as well as the deception and lies are ever more transparent, no matter how the people wish to unsee what is appearing. The call to all says "Wake Up." Wake up! Remember who you are.

It is an amazement to those who are long on the frontlines, but the youth pick up the torch quite easily. They are wise and see it is all a sham—a joke. They will reject the old ways of doing things. Those energy patterns will be no more.

Do not cling to anything from the past vibrations. That old ship has sailed and is now sinking beneath the waves of cosmic light. Swim, surf, float, but let go of the sinking wreck that can be no more.

The work now is in the emotional body—the water body where the metamorphosis occurs. Although you feel adrift in the cosmic seas, the currents have you in tow—the breath will fill you to buoy you up. There is nothing to fear. You will not drown here. It is a sea of love, and you will learn to breathe it in and out—like a fish with newly formed gills.

It is wonderful. Be full of the wonder and in gratitude for the grand beginning of the larger purpose, expanded viewpoint, and ascension, even though it is not what you expected. How could you foresee the glory of the higher dimensions when you have been perceiving with third-dimensional eyes?

Just see with new eyes with greater clarity and understanding. Just go with the flow of the cosmic winds of change. You are safe. You are held and rocked in the arms of the Great Love. That love that created all that is just for you, the children of the highest.

Accept your birthright, your heritage, and royalty in the house—the castle of your benevolent father/mother who are welcoming you home. They greet you with joy and thanksgiving, for you have been gone too long in the density of illusion. It is a very happy time.

We wish to encourage you on your journey. Enjoy all that is new as if an explorer having an adventure discovering new worlds. A curiousness will serve you. Be caught up in the awe and wonder of the depth of this unexplored ocean that is GOD. Be buoyed up by the magical synchronicities that continue to roll out the path before you.

Keep walking. Solid ground will appear, and you will learn to fly, to levitate, and more. All is well. Doubt not. We have you well in hand.

Just take that next step and the next. Even a blind man can do that. (Laughter.) You are supported. You are loved. NEVER doubt that. Angels attend you, so don't forget to invoke them for the support you need. For we love you with a true and lasting love always and forever.

We will not let you fall.

And so it is.

The Angels

Weather the Storm

As wings of light surround you, you can feel and accept the support of Heaven's messengers. The light that wishes to move through you in any way it can and at any time it can—even on short notice (laughing)—is ever present. There is no time of course, and we are with you in the ever present now.

Do not worry over the timing or even the message, because it is held in the vibration. The download of energy is transmitted with the words that you hear with inner knowing.

Each soul is able to tap into the flow of information pouring in from Source. So don't be surprised if the message is the same that another receives. It should only serve to let you know that you also have an ear to hear information that will be heard by everyone who will listen.

Of course, it takes practice to quiet the mind and let in the flow. The key is to be receptive and ready to receive. You can do it. It is simple. It is easy. The breath is the connection to source energy. Center in the core with your breath. Then you will feel it. Not seeking, not forcing—just be easy about it.

Humanity wants to do, do, do. But we caution you, busyness and trying too hard only gets in the way.

You want to know about the extreme weather that is happening in the United States and globally. The chaos and cataclysm of forces you cannot control have been attributed to God and his emissaries for centuries. However, these are natural cycles.

The Earth energy consciousness, sometimes called Gaia, *is cleansing all in her own way. Much of the destruction and death has been mitigated by prayer and calls to the angelic realm, for we always hear and answer, but much more adjustment is necessary to set the Earth spinning in the new energy patterns. This cannot be helped.*

Continue to help each other in compassion and kindness for all that has been lost or seems to be lost. What appears in the reality is channeled through your bodies that act as tuning forks and, as such, part of the energy field of Earth. You are not separate from it. Calming your own emotional body will do much to help the entire planet, and everyone makes a difference.

So much has been shifted by your belief and intention already. Good work! Continue onward in the same vein.

You cannot really understand what goes on in other dimensions when your senses only perceive in the third dimension. **But other senses and** *abilities are coming online. Be patient. Trust in the divine timing. All is well.*

And so it is.

The Angels

Tool #7 – Noticing Subtle Intuition Practice

We can develop and practice using physical and subtle (psychic or intuitive) senses to tune into angelic frequencies. These are often called the "Clairs"; each helps us receive divine guidance differently. You can begin to be more aware and awake to these:

1. Clairvoyance (Clear Seeing)

- **Sense Developed:** Inner vision
- **Practice:** Visualization, guided meditations, dream journaling
- **How it Helps:** You may see symbols, colors, flashes of light, or even angels in your mind's eye.

2. Clairaudience (Clear Hearing)

- **Sense Developed:** Inner and outer hearing
- **Practice:** Listening in silence, sound healing, tuning forks, music meditation
- **How it Helps:** You may hear divine guidance as a soft inner voice, channeled messages, or angelic music.

3. Clairsentience (Clear Feeling)

- **Sense Developed:** Emotional and physical sensitivity

- **Practice:** Body awareness exercises, breathwork, heart-centered meditation
- **How it Helps:** You feel an angelic presence through chills, tingling, or warm sensations—especially around the heart or shoulders.

4. Claircognizance (Clear Knowing)

- **Sense Developed:** Intuitive understanding
- **Practice:** Journaling, automatic writing, sitting with a question and receiving insight
- **How it Helps:** You just *know* things—truths drop into your awareness like divine downloads.

5. Clairalience (Clear Smelling) & Clairgustance (Clear Tasting)

- **Sense Developed:** Spiritual smell and taste
- **Practice:** Awareness through scent, taste, and memory triggers (e.g., smelling roses or incense with no physical source)
- **How it Helps:** These are subtle, but angels may communicate with floral scents or a sweet taste to indicate their presence or support.

Additional Practices to Strengthen These Senses:

- Spend time in silence and nature
- Use sacred sound (like Solfeggio tones)
- Practice calling in angels daily
- Create a sacred space
- Keep an "Angel Journal" to track experiences and insights.

List those extra senses you have experienced or those that you would like to cultivate and ask the angels for guidance.

_____

_____

_____

_____

_____

_____

_____

_____

_____

_____

_____

_____

_____

_____

_____

_____

_____

_____

_____

_____

_____

_____

_____

_____

_____

8

THE WORLD IN ASCENSION AND AWAKENING

*T*he angels talk of the Earth's ascension as the human collective awakens in consciousness. It is not an easy process. We have been experiencing many symptoms of this evolution for some time. There is no precise date when humanity will evolve sufficiently to unite consciousness.

The direction is to go within, release old ways of doing and being, and get comfortable with change and the unknown. To many, this feels like losing one's mind or dying the death of the ego. At any rate, we are going through it, and we have the help of our angels and guides to help us to do it with more ease and grace.

The opportunity is to master the frequencies of gratitude, love, and joy and live life in awe and wonder. There has never been more opportunity for glory and bliss. We are at the threshold. Although most of the messages here have not been published on my blog or made public before, this one has, and I have also shared it on my YouTube channel. I felt this message; we are at the place of prophetic changes and must make conscious choices.

Awaken—It's Game Over

The old habit of looking outside oneself for soothing answers is strong. Whatever is uncomfortable inside throws you under the bus again and again, so to speak. It is time to find comfort outside of your comfort zone. All is happening perfectly, and you will be safe enough in the unknown. It is part of the journey.

Develop the automatic reaction to go within instead of looking for comfort in food, in relationships, and in addictions of all kinds. They never satisfy. Like the old 60's song "(I Can't Get No) Satisfaction," your old ways of consoling yourself will not work anymore. Give them up! And the old energy patterns—give them up too.

Most people are in a state of craving more—more of everything and anything to shore up the ego identity. The programming of the mass consciousness is to get more to fill the void you are feeling. It will not work! It has never worked! Surrender to the direction of your guides and angels, and slip the track of the old cycles that loop around and around and take you nowhere.

Everyone must choose. You always have the freewill choice to cling to the sinking ship of dissatisfaction and disillusion of course, but why? Why would you choose that?

Becoming conscious shines light on the path before you. You are not in darkness unless you close your eyes and pretend you don't see. (Angel laughing.) How long do you want to play blind man's bluff and Marco Polo? These are children's games.

Turn to your guides and angels—they will answer. The path is much easier than you make it. Open your eyes. In fact, the path is like flowing down the stream—merrily, merrily, "life is but a dream" to quote another children's song. To choose anything else is just foolishness.

In fact, the Fool in the tarot card decks is the point of beginning—new beginnings. As we have told you again and again—now is a new beginning and will be every day until you are on solid ground with a new way of being in the world of form. You will soon forget the darkness, for it was never real. It has always been a game of duality where you closed your eyes to your identity. Just open them.

Awaken! There is no darkness after all but only the pretense of separation. Only oneness is real. Only love is real. Feel that reality NOW! Communicate that reality to all you meet on the path. Like you, they stumble. They lean on you for stability until they get tired of the game and open their eyes too.

Keep telling yourself, keep telling everyone, "Open your eyes—awaken!" Ask, listen, breathe, meditate, feel your feelings and then release them.

You are enough! You are whole! You are a divine being. And you are love in action. You are the creator of all you see and much more that you do not see yet. Much more will come into focus for you as the light of the new day dawns for all you earthlings. (More laughing.)

Wake up—stay awake. Olly olly oxen free. The jig is up. The game is over. You are free to come home.

And so it is.

The Angels

Note on my Blog: The Fool card in tarot is numbered 0—the number that stands for unlimited potential. The Fool's journey is the adventure through life. It is the journey that is ever present and, as such, needs no number.

"Olly olly oxen free" is a catchphrase used in children's games like capture the flag, kick the can, and hide and seek. It signals that hiding players can come into the open without losing the game or that the sides have changed, such as which team is in the field or who is up next or at bat in baseball or kickball. Many mothers also called out the phrase when the game was over, and it was time to go home for dinner.

Angel-Oracle Message for the New Age

Change is at the doorstep of the new year. Choose which changes you will make for the good of all mankind. Change stimulates the process of awakening. It provides the contrast, the friction necessary to produce the desire to clear the energy patterns of the past—those patterns that are lodged in the four lower bodies.

The consciousness that is awakening dislodges the denser energy that has stagnated in various ways. This produces a change in the circumstances perceived in the physical, because the physical is a representation of that energy matrix that is within.

In this density of the third dimension, it is perceived as a linear process, but in fact, there is no time in the eternal, and all is happening simultaneously. It seems that synchronicities happen more and more often because the gap between the linear perception of cause and effect is closing.

It is one of the signs that we are moving into fourth and fifth dimensions. The timeless nature of the reality we now begin to operate in allows the results of thought and feelings to materialize faster and faster.

This instant materialization can be wonderful and magical when there is beauty and light within. It can also be devastating as the ugliness and darkness become illuminated. The need to master one's thoughts and emotions becomes as evident as 2 + 2 = 4 or touching a hot stove.

There is not room for sloppiness in one's creative forces. Many ancient civilizations on Earth self-destructed when wielding this force inappropriately. This very nearly happened again in your lifetime, but for the intervention of advanced souls who were determined to hold the balance and transmute the darkness.

The shift in consciousness will now return to each person the material evidence of their thought patterns. This appears to some as the judgment—as the wrath of God—or karmic return. It is the physics of creation—the laws of cause and effect appearing in quantum fields.

The changes of circumstance will become radical as the energy stabilizes. Those who cannot or will not turn their attention inward to connect with Source—those who will not take responsibility for their creation—will terminate their existence on the Earth.

The Earth herself is in an ascension process. It is up to the individual to embrace the light and allow only light, peace, and happiness. No one can do it for you. It is a matter of survival as the evolution of humanity is happening. It is truly the age of the survival of the most loving!

Again, not because of judgment but of natural laws that are the physics of creation, you are the creator of your experience. You are the hands—the physical representation of Source energy.

Be wise—live life consciously! The result of sloppy or dark thoughts and deeds will continue to manifest very quickly in this change, and it will become painfully obvious who is responsible. There will be no place to hide from lack of integrity any longer.

Change will happen voluntarily or not. The Earth energies will be as a stove that becomes as hot as the refiner's fire. You will be "burned" children if you hold onto the hot stove. You must adapt to the changes.

Still your mind, and clear your emotional body. Purify the physical as well. Do this voluntarily, with wisdom and illumination, as the light and energy move matter to a faster frequency of energy.

*Do you understand? You do know this at a deep soul level. Allow the density to be released from you. You cannot hold onto it. **Be only light and love.***

We say this not to scare you but to point out that it is simply a choice like any other choice, and you make thousands every day. Be conscious of what you choose.

The results of the energy that you wield as creative power will be self-evident. Take responsibility for your own creation, for it is a wonderful, magical power. See it as such—use it as a great gift, and all will be well.

Calm the tempest within—release fear and "walk on the water" of the stormy seas of change with faith. We have spoken of this already. You can choose to enjoy the process. New beginnings are glorious. You are ready for a change! Choose with wisdom each and every thought.

Awaken—pay attention. The answer to your prayers for changes in the world are now being made manifest. The Earth and all thereon, down to the microcosm of the smallest fractal, will feel the shifting sands of physical reality slipping under you.

Be the peace that you seek! Be the port in the storm! You are the light! You are the love! We love you mightily and will hold you and guide you with each step—you have only to ask.

Ask, listen, and follow. It is easy! Let it be so for you.

Amen!

The Angels

Awaken to the Passion for Unity

You are the light—the light for those around you. Even though the way seems dark for you at times, hold on to what you feel in your soul and receive direction from the Holy Spirit.

The Holy Spirit is an essence of God energy that comes upon you to clarify the light within—to direct and bridge the gap of Heaven and Earth. It is a gap that seems to exist but is now only a small shift in perception.

The goal is to make the shift permanent—to bring Heaven into the body. Bringing the immensity of your soul into this plane of density transmutes all, like the alchemist who turns lead into gold. The consciousness that animates each cell comes into resonance and alignment with what is more love and joy.

The higher vibratory dimensions are only small adjustments of your receiving channel now. As you learn to change your frequency at will, the "heavens open" and the blessings pour out. What many perceive as "way up there" in a so distant Heaven is only a heartbeat away in the timeless. The veil of separation grows thinner still.

Quantum energy is not linear, and things that required time to make them happen in a denser, more sluggish energy now become manifested.

There is such a focus on manifesting your wishes for material things in this realm. It seems to be so challenging to become the creator here, and yet you create everything around you.

You love the challenge—the stretch required for the mastery of this elemental world. You can show off your skill in such a dramatic way and pronounce the greatest victory. And a remarkable victory it is—make no mistake! You, as humanity, have been long in the work of transformation. Many civilizations have come and gone in the attempt.

There have been the way-showers—the brighter lights who have come, like you, to pioneer the trail through the jungle of density. Great explorers are you.

Adventurers from higher realms and other worlds have been drawn here to uplift the very rocks of this place in third-dimensional time and space.

The soul of the planet Earth, Gaia, is awakened to the transformation, and elemental life has synchronized to the beat of a new drum.

The beat of the new drum awakens you to the passion for unity—to the call of oneness. It burns within the cells now and will not be stopped.

Release the floodgates of the unseen world of spirit. The light pours down upon you, and the heavens are opened in a deluge of the blessings that have been in storage for you for so long. They have been awaiting the right combination to unlock those rusty gates.

The pineal glands of awakening became petrified in the waiting. Now they vibrate and are changed by the dripping of the water of the Holy Spirit. The cave of understanding awakens with renewed life, and what seemed buried, entombed within you, is receiving the light.

It won't be long before the old way of petrified life will flow with ease and the dark days will be forgotten. After healing, the pain disappears, and soon it is remembered no more. Humanity is resilient in this way. Life is meant to change. Nothing remains the same after all—even in the densest of matter/energy.

Be lite and light now, and float on the breeze of new beginnings. The spring of a new age and the New Earth has come after a long sleep in winter. You may not see the growth of the flowers yet, but if you feel into the turn of the seasons, you can almost smell the spring of a new age.

Shake off the dirt, oh flower of life, and greet the Sun—the light of a new day dawning.

And so it is.

The Angels

I love the poetry of the angels and how they use metaphors, analogies, and other story forms to get the message across. The following message started very differently in a letter format. I am always delighted, surprised, and deeply moved by many of the unexpected things that appear in the messages. After writing these messages by hand, I gradually learned to type them without allowing my mental chatter to interrupt or change them. After years of typing them in a blog format, I have again changed to be more efficient. I now experiment with just speaking them as dictation because I have more practice keeping my ego mind out of the mix.

Oneness: Unity Consciousness

Dear World of One,

The heart sings with the victory of Earth's ascension cycle. There was so much hope that this timeline would be the one that free will would ultimately choose. The unknown ingredient makes everything more spicy, interesting, and exciting.

It's all about the infinite possibilities and humanity choosing the life path most in alignment in frequency to your own desires.

In this scenario, you are ahead of schedule, and the Universe is joyous in celebration and eager to aid in the transition to fourth- and fifth-dimensional consciousness.

Those of you who are done with the density of the third-dimensional experience are so ready to move on. That old energy is just falling away like the dried-up snakeskin that is left in the woods.

The Magic of Awakening

Being awake to the magic of existence is to notice the creative force in ALL THAT IS. Awaken to the beauty of the designs of life that abound on the Earth and beyond. Notice the beauty of the repeating patterns of love.

You can have what you wish for, ask for, believe in, and adore. Just let it in! Heaven supports you in all of it! In fact, it is the premise of the grand experiment of being third-dimensional, and you chose to have it that way. All was created for you just as you ordered it.

Yes, it is in ORDER! Do not doubt that everything is the unfoldment of your awakening as creator.

You want to know what is the meaning in this? Where is the fun? We say—if you aren't having fun, don't do it! You have freewill choice in everything. You are only imprisoned by the mind that thinks it has to keep you safe in your chosen straightjacket.

There is no need for safety—not in the way that you think—for you are eternal, and God loves you truly. Rest in knowing that. You do know it at the core of your being—let that love in!

You have only to let it in! Release the judgment. Release the judgment of Self, of others, and enjoy the journey.

Seriously—it can and will be the way you design it for the greatest good of all. Trust that! Feel safe in knowing that the Great I AM holds you in the arms of eternal love. This is truth and the only reality. All else is an illusion of separation that is unraveling with exposure to the solvent of love and light.

Relax, have fun with the shifting of reality—for it is a unique experience you, and all beings for that matter, have awaited and hoped for. The transition will be over before you know it, and this phase of human existence will blend into the tapestry of creative forces beyond your understanding.

There is no reason NOT to enjoy all of it! Resistance is futile! (Laughing out loud.)

"Let go and let God," as they say . . . be happy with that! For you see, all IS PERFECT!

Only love is real. ONLY LOVE.

And so it is.

The Angels

"Resistance is futile" is a common phrase in popular culture. It comes from the first encounter between humans and the Borg in the second season of the series *Enterprise* in the episode "Regeneration," where they state, "You will be assimilated; resistance is futile." It was also used in the *Star Wars* movies, spoken by Darth Vader. This is rather off-putting to us because the idea of losing our identity in assimilation is so repulsive. The angels affirm that Oneness we experience is not to be confused with the technological simulation of our spiritual ascension process. I alert you here so you do not get confused by this.

Resistance to the evolution of higher consciousness and cosmic energies of entering into the Age of Aquarius is not only futile because of the magnitude of the energies and the power of love and light momentums at play, but is also painful. The angels speak about the joy of releasing the layers of density and claiming a new reality in the following message. My experience of

Oneness was so awesomely beautiful that it has been compared to a Near Death Experience (NDE) of being in heaven. I assure you that the amount of love awaiting us is nothing to fear.

The Joy of Ascension

How great is the joy of a higher vibration! How wonderful to awaken in a new reality! Claim it as your own. It is a reflection of that light that resonates with the new circuitry in your form.

The joy you feel is just the beginning. You have successfully peeled back the layers of density that were weighing you down. It's a new beginning for you, for us, for all—the leading edge of a dream that is breaking out of third-dimensional reality.

The natural world vibrates at a new level, too. Can you enjoy this and soak it in? It's like floating in a hot spring—a spring of natural water bubbling up from the earth.

Join the host of souls in the ascension vortex and continue to rise. You can see it in your mind's eye. Do not look back. Others will be pulled up in the fabric of the web that all are attached to, like jewels of dew on a spider's web. Up and up. Oh JOY.

You have the tools, the motivation, the vision, the light, and the support team to make a difference. Your body will also follow. Be light—and lite!

And so it is. Amen.

The Angels

These messages from the angels show that we have what it takes to jump to the next dimension. We have tools and the assistance of multidimensional beings. Their messages empower and encourage me, and I hope they do the same for you.

Here is the finale of the tools and practices for integrating with the angels and bringing their energy into the world as embodied light. You are always loved and supported.

Tool #8 – Embodying Angelic Qualities: Becoming the Living Light

Integrating angelic attributes means consciously awakening and reflecting the virtues that angels represent, such as unconditional love, divine wisdom, compassion, strength, purity, and forgiveness. This makes you a living conduit of their frequencies and purpose on Earth.

Signs You're Integrating Angelic Energy

- You become more emotionally balanced and compassionate.

- Your intuition sharpens and decisions feel divinely guided.

- Others feel peaceful or uplifted in your presence.

- You are less reactive and more heart-centered.

4 Steps on the Path of Integration – Embodying Angelic Energy

1. **Intention & Invocation:** You practice inviting the angels to guide your soul's evolution. Next, call in specific Archangels to infuse you with their light (e.g., Michael for

strength, Raphael for healing, Chamuel for divine love). You can take a course in the Archangels listed at the end of this book.

2. **Daily Alignment Practices:** You use tools like morning rituals, affirmations, and breathwork to raise your vibration to align with the angelic realms. Visualize yourself filled with the color rays as energies of heavenly light. Ask yourself, "How would an angel act in this situation?" Practice patience, presence, nonjudgment, and higher compassion moment by moment.

3. **Sacred Service:** You move with mindfulness to serve from love, not ego. Embody the attributes of angels through selfless acts, healing, listening, or simply being a peaceful presence.

4. **Receiving & Radiating Grace:** You accept divine help by being open to miracles. Then, you radiate this energy to others by silently blessing them, praying, or holding light for them.

Angelic Embodiment Affirmation:

"I am a vessel of divine light, love, and wisdom. With every breath, I embody the radiant qualities of the angels and shine them into the world."

Tune into your higher self and imagine your body surrounded in light and love with angelic colors and radiance. Breathe this light into the central core of your body and breathe out more love expanding it into the world.

CONCLUSION

The Rest of the Story

So, we conclude this collection of angel messages that started my work with the angelic realms. I finally feel confident that the messages and the number of people who hear them will keep coming. Communicating with the angels transforms me, and I know you have been changed too. When we invoke divine help to receive, we open the channel for many blessings to flow to us and through us, for the benefit of all.

As I allow myself to be seen and to "come out" as an angel communicator and publish this book, it opens the way and possibility for you to do the same. The larger truth is that we are all connected to higher powers and will evolve in our intuitive gifts. The angels want you to know that cultivating your connection to Source is most important. It is never lost. Divine guidance is always available in many forms; attune to the messages for more peace and happiness.

Angels and many other beings of light await you to reach out to them. At the level of your Highest Self, we are truly one with the Source—the ALL THAT IS. You are loved so much more than you will ever know. Allow this to be true for you. Become ONE with that love.

ANGELIC AND SPIRITUAL AWAKENING GLOSSARY

Angels

Celestial beings created by the Divine to serve as messengers, protectors, and helpers of humanity. Angels are beings of pure light and love, supporting us on our soul's journey and guiding us through divine intuition and inspiration.

Archangel

A high-ranking angel overseeing vast aspects of spiritual evolution. Archangels work with universal energies and are guardians of the divine rays. Each Archangel embodies a particular frequency of light and spiritual attribute, like healing, strength, wisdom, or love.

Archangel Michael

Known as the Angel of Protection, Strength, and Divine Will. Michael carries the Blue Flame of Power and is called upon to cut away fear, negativity, and cords that bind. He helps us stand in our truth, release lower patterns, and protect our spiritual path.

Archangel Gabriel

The Messenger of God and Angel of Revelation, Purity, and Clarity. Gabriel brings divine messages, helps us hear our soul's calling, and inspires creativity, communication, and new beginnings.

Channeling

Channeling is the spiritual practice of receiving messages or divine energy from higher realms, such as angels, ascended masters, or one's higher self. Angelic channeling brings loving, supportive, and often healing messages for spiritual growth and guidance.

Spiritual Awakening

A process of remembering who you truly are beyond the physical self. It is the unfolding of awareness, intuitive gifts, and divine connection. During awakening, people become more attuned to angelic guidance and the unseen realms of spirit.

Ascension

The expansion of consciousness occurs when a person embodies more of their soul's light, raises their vibration, and aligns with their higher spiritual purpose. It is a personal and planetary shift toward unity, love, and divine truth. Angels assist us in this evolution.

New Age

A spiritual movement focused on personal transformation, universal love, holistic healing, and metaphysical awareness. It embraces tools like angelic communication, energy healing, meditation, and intuitive development.

Intuitive Guidance

Messages from the soul, spirit guides, or angels that are felt through inner knowing, sensation, visions, or sudden insight. Strengthening intuitive guidance is key to receiving angelic help and aligning with your higher path.

Spirit Guides

Non-physical beings are assigned to assist each soul on their life journey. These may include ancestral spirits, animal totems, ascended masters, or angelic beings. They offer wisdom, protection, and gentle nudges toward your highest path.

The 7 Archangels - major Archangels organized as Seven Rays of Divine Light:

Michael – 1st Ray: Will, Protection, Power (Blue)

Jophiel – 2nd Ray: Wisdom and Illumination (Yellow-Gold)

Chamuel – 3rd Ray: Love and Adoration (Pink)

Gabriel – 4th Ray: Purity and Harmony (White)

Raphael – 5th Ray: Healing and Truth (Green)

Uriel – 6th Ray: Peace and Service (Ruby-Gold)

Zadkiel – 7th Ray: Transformation and Forgiveness (Violet)

Thank You

Thank you for your attention to the messages from the angels in this book.

There are many ways to connect with more of the angels, archangels, and other beings of light. To find the most recent Angel-Oracle Messages, visit my website, where you can also receive free meditations, energy transmissions, activations, and many years of blog posts.

Free Gift
A beautiful eBook of *"Real Angel Blessings,"*
10 Archangel blessings plus a list of the
Archangels with their expertise.
And weekly channeled Angel Messages like those in the book.

lindsaygodfree.com/newsletter-subscribe
(Unsubscribe at any time)

Join my social media groups and participate in
the discussion. Don't hesitate to reach out.

Schedule a Free Zoom Consultation:
consult.lindsaygodfree.com

ACKNOWLEDGMENTS

I am grateful for the angels' intercession in my life. They have taught me to accept help. I made life so hard by going it alone most of my life. I thought that if I had any help, then I was cheating, and I couldn't count my accomplishments. It was a very limiting way to live.

I have many people to thank for supporting me in finishing this book, as well as the teachers and organizations that taught me about spirituality. The angels pushed me to expand myself and let other people in.

First, I want to acknowledge my six daughters, who taught me love and expanded my heart to overflow whenever I think of them. During my years of depression, they gave me reasons to carry on and to aspire to be a good example of persistence in following one's dreams.

I want to acknowledge my mother, Suzanne, who provided the finances to publish this book and often supported me and my angel classes.

I am thankful for my travel and driving partner, John, who never complains about all the many hours I spend doing my angel work. Although he is a nonbeliever in spiritual things, he believes in me.

I want to acknowledge my friend Tamera, who has believed in this project and has been effusive in her praise for my books and angel messages. She has always been my biggest fan and first to read and purchase all my offerings.

I am grateful for my early teachings in the Mormon Church, which taught me that it is possible to speak to angels, and they have and still do appear to people on Earth.

I learned about archangels and grew to know them through the Summit Lighthouse teachings and channeled messages. My explanation of angels and archangels reflects many of those ideas.

I also want to mention Dr. Sue Morter, whose teachings about energy frequencies and building circuitry to hold and expand the divine energy we are as beings of light have been invaluable.

My friend Susan graciously gifted me her skill in editing my books. She has been a true friend for years and deserves many blessings for her giving heart.

I am thankful for my book writing group in the Authors Success Academy and Shanda of Transcendent Publishing for her teachings and ongoing support in taking the books to the finish line of best-selling authors.

I acknowledge all of you who are awakening, believe in angels, and can live a magical and mystical life. I thank you for your support!

ABOUT THE AUTHOR

Lindsay Godfree is an intuitive channeler who writes a blog of Angel-Oracle Messages. Author of the best-selling book, ***Awakening Consciousness: Discovering a Larger Version of Self***, and creator of the Consciousness Guide. Lindsay is a certified sound therapy practitioner, facilitator of The Energy Codes with the Morter Institute for Bioenergetics, and a spiritual life coach certified by the Transformational Academy.

Lindsay lives in Arizona and is the mother of six beautiful and accomplished daughters.

Lindsay offers personal channeled messages and transmissions from the angelic realm, tuning your energy to the frequencies of higher consciousness. On her website, you can purchase Angel-Oracle Readings, Personal Channeled Readings, meditations, and eBooks. You can also subscribe for free Weekly Channeled Messages, a Quarterly Newsletter, special offers, and free gifts at www.lindsaygodfree.com.

Look for the live and online transformational course based on her book on awakening consciousness and an in-depth masterclass regarding the 7-Archangels called ***Bathe in the Love of the Angels***. For information, email her at lindsay@lindsaygodfree.com.